Serving To Your Own and Others' Penance

Anxiety's Back Story
Change the stories of your past to be
free to fly!

By Edie Gardner, LCSW, CPA

Serving To Your Own and Others' Penance
Copyright © 2020 by Edie Gardner, LCSW, CPA

IMPORTANT DISCLAIMER: This book is designed not to trigger unexplored areas or not to be a hinderance to healing. This book is also not designed to be a diagnostic tool. This book is to point out commonalities that I have observed among anxiety sufferers and not as any kind of replacement for therapy. Reviewing your story is not easy work. If you have suffered from trauma in your past, I strongly encourage you to work with a therapist trained in trauma recovery while healing from your past.

Dedication

This book is dedicated to the riders on the self-improvement bus.

C'mon. Join us.

I consider myself thin because that is how I spread myself.

I consider myself an author, even before this book, because I wrote the book on guilt.

This book is one person's travel guide, one path on the journey out of the forest of anxiety. You have to find your customized road out of this forest. I hope this book helps you carve your own path. I can tell you that the destination is a peace of mind that is nothing short of Heaven on earth.

Introduction

Like a magician who asks you to pick a card, any card, I ask you to pick a problem, any problem, before starting this book.

My theory is that your current problem has deep roots from where you have been in the past. Almost every problem has an emotional component. Learn your emotional reaction to the stories of your past first. Then, you are ready to change those reactions so that your past is working for you.

Wouldn't it be incredible if you turned your baggage from the past into healing tools of lessons for your best future ever?

Part I: Understanding the Past's Prison

Chapter One: Traveling Back in Time

Bucket lists are goals of the soul. My main bucket list item at one time was to experience all fifty states before I reached fifty years old. While I accomplished this fifty-state journey, I had no idea the journeys that would open afterwards because of where I have been previously.

I don't know why I was surprised that my previous journeys would affect my current situation. I have long understood that where we have been in the past shapes everything on how we view the world today. Vacations can cost a lot of money up front, but the benefits of past vacations can live on in our memories. We can learn how to travel back in time. Not all return trips are as happy as vacations, but you will learn here how to make your return trips extraordinarily valuable.

This book is a travel journal because you are going to retrace your past steps. We are going to travel back in time frequently. Think of me as your travel agent on these trips. The best travel agents have traversed the paths already and have experienced the destinations. I have retraced my steps and have found the roots of current problems. Many times, the terrain is rough in retracing your steps, but the destination is a freedom to be yourself, to not hide your beauty, and to celebrate your uniqueness. By giving yourself the tools that you previously sought from others, you now will serve your purpose. You will learn how to give naturally and not from obligation. You will come to learn how anxiety might just be one of the greatest roads to true freedom to fly.

Odds are exceedingly high that your current problems have roots in the stories of your past. Through these look back journeys, you will transform your pain from the past into your greatest tools. When we go

on a journey, we pack bags. By working through emotional reactions to the stories of your past, you will learn how to travel into the future with beautiful bags of tools instead of baggage. You are here to resolve how anxiety is manifesting in your life. Welcome to the journey back in time. Anxiety can become a window of opportunity for exponential growth.

Pick your top, #1 problem in your world right now that you would like to work on throughout this book's journey. Before you commit your problem to paper, make sure you are defining it solely as YOUR problem because then you can find YOUR solution. For example, let's say you define your problem as a lack of productivity with your department at work largely because your staff is inefficient. If the problem is defined that way, the solution depends on others' actions. If you define the problem instead as your inability to communicate work expectations and to address conflicts, the solution is in your control as you will be addressing your behaviors. The bad news is that you have to do the work yourself; the good news is that you do not have to depend on others. When you realize you ultimately only have control of yourself, you learn how to stay in your own lane for the solutions.

As you travel with me on your path to reshape anxieties' back stories, here are my rules of the road:

1. These look backs at your past self have to be done while being exceptionally kind to yourself. You have tried it your way of beating yourself up for your past, and now please try it my way by showing yourself grace and self-forgiveness. You are going to hear "grace and self-forgiveness" a lot in this book.

2. We are not going to be changing the facts of what happened in the past, but we are going to be reshaping your lenses of how you see past stories.

3. Loyalty is one of my top values in life. With that said, many times clients feel they are being disloyal to loved ones by describing how they have been hurt by others. Please know that in order to get to the sources of your real pain, you have to tell the story first. It is very difficult to forgive someone until you fully understand what you are forgiving. Most times we have carried pain with us for a long time, and in a way, the images in our heads of people take on a life of their own. We usually have isolated a few painful events when we think of some people who have wronged us. By traveling with the pain associated with certain people we forget their essence and their goodness. They become all bad in our minds unless we address the source of pain. By revising our vision of the pain and our emotional reactions, we are able to let go and forgive others. You are not being disloyal to carve a path of forgiveness.

4. Let me save you some time. You are not selfish or lazy. Energy spent labeling yourself this way does not help motivate you. It perpetuates the pattern of being held back from being true to yourself. Playing small has worked for others and maybe even for you in the past, but it is time to tell a new story by letting go of labels that are just holding you back.

5. The only way for this process to work is by being completely honest with yourself. Judging yourself is just one more way of keeping you down. Bringing your most authentic self to this process will help to peel back the surface layers to get to the real issues.

6. Feelings matter, and yet when we deny, numb, or repress them, the feelings do not disappear. That energy still exists. Pressure is created, and that pressure will be released in unhealthy ways if healthy ways are not allowed. If you are exhausted, it is likely an emotional exhaustion of putting on pretenses and creating an

outer identity that others see. This is a false persona. You can change your feelings by changing your thought patterns, but you cannot "wish away" feelings through denial, numbing, or repression.

Is this the right time to work toward feeling better about the stories from your past? On a scale of 1-10, how committed are you to feeling better? If you did not score 8-10, I appreciate your honesty.

First figure out what is keeping you from fully committing to this process. This is a really important step because a lower score probably means you are really scared to let go of how you have been processing the past. That is okay! Previous thought patterns did their job and protected you, but now these same thought patterns may be more of the problem than the solution.

This travel journey is to teach you how to feel free enough to fly. You are learning how to transform your pain from the past into the greatest of lessons. Honesty is really the only path to true freedom. It is a must that you come to this journey honestly. It is a judgment-free zone here, but it really only works if you are honest with yourself.

Let's start wherever you are.

Chapter Two: The Ultimate Top Ten List

Do you have your #1 problem plaguing you right now, the problem where you need the most relief? I do not know your issue, but let me give you ten ingredients on how this issue has likely become as big as it has:

1. Perfectionism: You are unable to let go of the problem because you will only feel resolution once you solve the problem completely, by doing it perfectly.

2. People Pleaser: You feel compelled to place others' expectations ahead of your own. You believe that by having others pleased with you, your work, or what you do, that happiness will be mirrored back to you. An extreme focus to please others has been labeled as honorable and faithful service. Since focusing on one's own needs has been labeled as selfish, pleasing others is part of one's faithful mission to be unselfish. When working toward your own goals seems so negative, resentment and giving solely out of a sense of obligation can result.

3. Procrastination: You are exceptionally hard on yourself to be the FIXER of EVERYTHING. Therefore, your agenda is rarely considered while you are working on accomplishing others' agendas. You rarely feel finished, and even when you allow yourself to relax, you are stealing that time away from truly relaxing by feeling guilty the whole time. It is a misnomer to call it free time because it is anything but free from guilt. You accept others' requests that overstep your boundaries, but then procrastination is a way for you to gain some control back in return. It is usually labeled as passive aggressive behavior, but the procrastination is an effort to regain your boundaries. Some credit should be given for honoring yourself.

4. Pain of the Past: Your current problem is likely a trigger to unresolved pain from your past. The subconscious mind stores memories by feelings and not by time. That is why current pain can be associated to events from long ago.

5. Heightened Sense of Responsibility: Not only do you have a strong sense of responsibility for yourself, but that responsible nature spills over into feeling dysfunctionally responsible for others' problems or feelings. This top ten list has been created because of the common symptoms I have found, but this heightened sense of responsibility is the most common and the most difficult to overcome. Usually people have gained such a sense of purpose and meaning by being hyper-responsible that it seems odd to be asked to sacrifice it.

6. Lack of Boundaries: Forming emotional boundaries is exceptionally difficult for you to justify. The word "No" is rarely used with others, which further overwhelms you and your to do list.

7. Extreme Expectations: Your self-expectations are so strong that it is easy to feel resentment and envy when others do not expect as much of themselves. "Hard on self" is one of the main descriptions you would give yourself. Usually, these extreme expectations spill over into expecting a lot from others too. Lowering any expectations feels dangerous because there is the fear that relaxing expectations will lead to severely reduced productivity.

8. Martha Stewart of Crafting Slightest Hint of Criticism: You are so in tune with recognizing even a hint of criticism in the outside world, and soon you have spun that hint into a monumentally exaggerated, internal argument of your ineptness. Your mind has

been focused on any outside dangers to threaten your security, but your mind has completely distorted the reality of an outside threat. You are likely highly intuitive to others and situations. You are able to "read" the energy of a room well. Unfortunately, you usually blame yourself for the negative energy or at least feel responsible for fixing the negativity.

9. Negative Self-Talk: Long-established patterns of negative thoughts are so ingrained into your mind that they are part of your subconscious, automatic thinking. Once you increase listening to the self-talk, you become aware of how pervasive this negative thinking has become. Once it is in your conscious world though, you are able to reshape it and to set yourself free.

10. Control: If only you could be completely in control of the situation, you could easily fix it. Anxiety sufferers usually like to be able to setup and control their environment. I commonly hear that they prefer to be alone because the pressure is off when they are left to themselves to set the rules. A sense of complete control means that the person does not have to worry about pleasing anyone else but themselves. Like a heightened sense of responsibility, a sense of control can spill over into controlling others.

Starting with the story of your current problem, go through each of these ten ingredients to see how these areas resonate. Then, try to piece together how these patterns have developed throughout your life, probably beginning in childhood. The third part is to find ways to work within your uniqueness and your strengths to overcome and rethink these ten ingredients. Finally, come up with a new and different way to view the solution to your problem.

This is about the time that I would like to hand you a cup of one of your favorite teas. T.E.A.S. is my acronym for Tell Edie A Story. Let's start with your current problem. We will work backwards until we can move forward again. Let's go.

Chapter Three: Free to Fly

"All of them." That is usually what my clients say when I describe my formula for anxiety and ask which parts resonate. Even though I keep adding to my formula, the main issues are about Control, Responsibility, and Service. By the end of this book, you will have four ways of feeling freer, no matter what the problem is. You will be free by:

1. Trusting your gut enough to have your instincts be a welcome part of the decision-making process,

2. Telling the truth and creating an environment of honesty,

3. Being responsible for yourself solely, and

4. Seeing your value (and others' value too) in who you ARE instead of only by what you do. Ironically, when you focus on your goodness, what you do gets better and better.

The relief that clients feel is almost palpable when they get more and more comfortable in their own, unique skin. When they stop putting on heirs, stop living up to others' expectations, stop trying to control how others see them (which they can't control by the way), and accept the good and bad parts of themselves, the pressure to be other than they naturally are is released. Even though I repeat it over and over again about honesty and being true to themselves, I can tell when it really sinks into their souls. Self-confidence and self-esteem naturally improve. When we value who we are, self-discipline comes naturally instead of being sacrificial and instead of merely being on our "should do" lists.

Your future travels will happen with the true you in the driver's seat. Your future problems will be eased by lessons from your past instead of being held back from the pain of your past. You will still need to return to the past to clear it, but you will do so with gifts of grace and self-forgiveness.

Chapter Four: The Creeper

I had one of my first counseling clients. I read their intake form and why they were seeking therapy. We worked on their problem. Soon I realized why they came in was only slightly related to the issue we were addressing. Their real problem was a lot deeper and had to do a lot with the past. Interesting.

My next client contracted with me. Hmmm, their issue sounded kind of familiar. It was a totally different scenario and problem, but the feelings resembled what the previous client described. Before I knew it, we were talking about their past. How did we get here? The way they solved their past problems wasn't working now. Why?

The next client began their intake form with, "I think I've been suffering from anxiety all my life." Hey, that's what my other clients said and exactly that way. Plus, all of these feelings they are describing ring true for my story. How can that be? Uh-oh, they warned us about countertransference in school. Maybe I better get my story straight, my issues worked out.

And so on and so on. Most of the clients I was seeing had some version of the same story. To work on their current problem, we were traveling back in time a lot. We were discussing previous coping methods, previous pain, and a ton about negative self-talk. I kept seeing myself in their stories. We all seemed to be part of a secret club of sensitive, hugely responsible people who were suffering. It was kind of like our minds were working against us now. Our minds had been so great at protecting us in the past, but now the same thoughts just didn't seem to be working. It just cannot be a coincidence (in which I don't believe) that we had the same pain.

In 1994, there was a celebration dinner in Las Vegas. The six dinner guests were given $200 each to gamble away. The group was celebrating their last weekend being anonymous. The next week was the pilot release of Friends. Six friends together experienced an instant transition from anonymity to incredible fame. The ten-year experience was different for each of the six with varied life experiences; some married, and some even had children during those ten years. Yet, those six were the only ones who really knew what it was like to be a famous friend. I imagine those six have a secret code or look they share. They have an incredible bond of having been through something huge together. No one else really knows what it is like to be one of the super six. (I have had a recurring dream that I was the lesser known seventh friend. I lived farther than Phoebe, and the six were always doing stuff without me. I am ostracized even in my own dreams!)

That is kind of how I think of anxiety sufferers' bond but without the $200 gambling money and the fame. As you will soon find in this book, I think of myself as a Truth Detective. From being hated as a public auditor to numerous social settings where there was a lot of phoniness and smoke and mirrors, I have learned about the healing power and value of the truth.

Even though there are many different forms of anxiety, there are many similarities too. That is why diagnosticians have grouped disorders together. It has been my experience that anxiety sufferers have been through a similar process. Each person's experience has been unique, as were the super six's life experiences, but there seem to be some quite common feelings too. Anxiety sufferers, like the super six, have a bond or a secret code. I think it is time to crack the code for all to feel free to be our truest selves.

I am on a mission to give people a blueprint to solve their own REAL problems. The current problem, my friend, is probably just the surface problem. The starting point is recognizing the stories of the past and how you have processed the meaning of life from those stories. I feel a strong connection to others who have suffered from self-imposed limitations. I think there is a formula to anxiety, and I am out to prove there is a formula for its mastery too.

I call anxiety the Creeper. Unless you recognize the common attributes of anxiety, it can creep into all unsuspecting crevices of your life. I have created a formula to identify these symptoms and to bring them to the light of day, out of our subconscious and automatic reactions. A whole lot less creeping can happen in broad daylight, in our conscious minds.

As a child, I lived on a quiet street with lots of children on the block, and we played a street game called Around the Block. One person on a bike rode up and down the street, and the object of the game was to get around the block without being seen by the bike rider. This rider was allowed only three "Look Backs" in the game. The rider had to perfectly time when to look back and had to make sure the Look Backs were not wasted.

You are likely going to find yourself looking back to your past a lot during and after reading this book. These look backs can only be wasted if you are not exceptionally kind to your past self. Please do not be the judge and jury now on how you protected yourself from pain. You learned thought patterns that might not be working well now, but they were highly effective then. I am going to help you to stop condemning yourself for how you protected yourself in the past. Your previous protection measures worked because they got you to this point. Now, you have picked up this book to further help yourself. You are ready to let go of the anxiety, to let go of the pain from the past, and to live freely.

Chapter Five: Handling the Truth

"I went to a restaurant that serves 'breakfast at any time." So, I ordered French Toast during the Renaissance."
— Steven Wright

In June of 1974, Jack Nicholson's movie Chinatown was about to be released. There is usually quite a bit of press to promote a new movie, and this was no exception. Jack was scheduled to take a telephone interview with a Time magazine reporter. I imagine celebrities are used to being asked questions that have nothing to do with their upcoming movie and everything to do with their fame, but still I imagine the reporter's question must have seemed out of the blue. The reporter asked Mr. Nicholson for his reaction to being raised by his mother and living with his sisters to only find out after childhood that in fact one of his sisters was actually his mother. Who he thought was his mother in childhood was actually his grandmother. His reaction? Well, at first there was a long pause. Jack was thirty-seven years old at the time, and that phone interview was the first time Jack had heard the family secret.

This reporter had done quite extensive research and uncovered a deep secret. His "mother"/grandmother and "sister"/mother were deceased by the time of the interview, but afterwards, Jack was able to confirm the news with his other "sister" who actually was his aunt. Jack took it in stride though. This was his reaction:

"I'd say it was a pretty dramatic event, but it wasn't what I'd call traumatizing... After all, by the time I found out who my mother was, I was pretty well psychologically formed. As a matter of fact, it made quite a few things clearer to me. If anything, I felt grateful."
— Jack Nicholson
Source:
https://www.thevintagenews.com/2018/08/22/jack-nicholsons-mother/

I am sure the next few years of Jack Nicholson's down, private time alone were spent reconstructing his past. I think his response is very gracious. During his childhood, he must have had incidences that made him question things about his family, and yet he probably just stuffed those observations down as something peculiar about himself. He probably grew up questioning his own abilities to interpret life because things were not adding up. He was taught subconsciously to ignore observations that did not make sense to him. Once the secret was out, I hope that he learned that his powers of observations should no longer be ignored. I hope he has learned to trust his gut.

We all should learn to trust our gut. The angriest I have been at various times of my life were actually anger with myself at not trusting what I knew to be true. What in your life just does not make sense to you?

Jack Nicholson's story is not all that unique. As it turns out, the singer Bobby Darin had quite a similar story. Though a famous singer, Bobby Darin was considering a career in politics. In 1968 at thirty-two years old, Mr. Darin learned that his sister was actually his mother. She had to reveal the truth out of fear it would come out while running for a political office.

(https://www.snopes.com/fact-check/you-dont-know-jack/)

Jack Nicholson's and Bobby Darin's stories are celebrity versions of the many family secrets that exist. As we have learned from Brene Brown's extensive research, shame thrives on lies. The end result of most lies is that children can learn to not trust their own observations and their own gut knowledge. That is the biggest crime from secrecy.

Secrets kill, but...

The truth sets you free.

Secrets are people's arrogance at thinking they can manipulate the natural order of life. When you lie to others, you are lying to yourself that you are more powerful than the truth.

No matter what facts change from your past, the absolute truth that remains pure is your reactions, meaning, and impressions of YOUR past. No one can take that away from you. No secret can be revealed to you that changes how you reacted. This book hopefully will help you to see that what is most important to your well-being is how you've processed your past. If the solutions to your current problems remain a mystery, odds are you can look to what is still troubling you about the stories of your past. As you will learn in this book, I have solved many personal and professional current problems by looking at the real problems of how I processed the meaning of my past. Let me show you how to use your past for your best future.

Even though others can't remove your reactions, YOU have the power to change those reactions if you wish. Most people think they want to change the past, but when they cannot, they blame others. Not letting go is usually because there is a benefit to seeing their past that way. If you are able to do the work to remove unhealthy reactions to pain from your past, you can be set free.

Chapter Six: Penance

"I was taking care of myself before I met you. You were taking care of yourself before you met me. Let's continue down this same path. Let's be together separately. But, he would come home and say stuff to me that I just didn't understand. 'Uh, what's for dinner?' 'I don't know. What'd you cook? I ate already.' 'I'm all out of clean underwear.' 'Ooooh. Then you need to do your laundry. I did mine yesterday. See? I have a whole drawer of clean panties. You are welcome to borrow a pair to tie you over if you'd like.'"
— Wanda Sykes

S.T.O.P. is my acronym for Serving To (your own and) Others' Penance. This book had to be this title. It is one of the main reasons I insisted on self-publishing because I knew a publisher was going to make me change the title. I was so tired of the perplexed looks when I told people the title of my book. The title was so descriptive for me, so clear, so packed with meaning. Yet, everyone who heard my title would simply say, "That's nice, Edie," or something with a lack of sincerity or perplexed look. Friends did not really want to admit that they did not understand the meaning of my title. And, then, one day I off-handedly told a friend the title and waited for her confused look. She stopped what she was doing and just said, "Wow." She totally got it. I believe that those who are still plagued by the prison walls of their past get the title and the full meaning behind it. Don't worry though if you don't understand the meaning yet because I will explain it fully.

The title of the book was going to simply be Serving To Others' Penance. However, I found that in addition to serving others' penance, most of my clients are unable to free themselves of their own past sins. Even outside of my counseling practice, I seem to attract people who are confessing their sins of the distant past to me. In my practice, I keep seeing people who cannot seem to let go of their childhood responsibilities and self-assigned blame for adult conflicts. Just one's very existence has been the root of all problems for many! I am very familiar with that self-blame and self-labeling as all bad, the source of all problems. I was only able to let go of that horrific pain once I realized I would have to be superhuman in order to be the cause of all pain. I did not want to consider myself as bigger or better than anyone else. After I committed to seeing myself as not superhuman, I was able to let go of the need to solve others' problems. Once I realized I could let go of that title of all bad, I set myself on a course of true freedom.

From an extensive, wonderful Catholic education, I learned that God forgives our sins. This is how it works in the Roman Catholic tradition. You enter the reconciliation room either facing your priest or entering behind a screen to maintain your anonymity. "Bless me, Father, for I have sinned," is how you begin. After confessing your sins, the priest gives you a penance which is usually a few prayers that you are to say right after reconciliation. But, the forgiveness has already been granted. by our Heavenly Father. This is how Catholics have been taught throughout history. I am a believer that God forgives, but something was wrong.

Though I have been taught that God forgives, it was the self-forgiveness that plagued me. There just never seemed to be enough penance for me to serve. I was constantly serving penance for the past. A few Hail Mary's and Our Father's just did not seem to erase the guilt.

But, the odd thing is that most of what plagued me was not really my own sins but my sense of responsibility for others' problems. I felt responsible for everything. The comedian Richard Lewis had a routine where he blamed himself for everyone else's problems. "The Beatles are breaking up? I could have bought more records. The Dodgers lost? I should have worn a blue shirt." Not only was that me, but I have found that most anxiety sufferers have the same dysfunctional sense of responsibility for other people's problems.

Let's make sure in everything that we do every day that we S.T.O.P serving penance for an inflated sense of responsibility (more on that later) for others' problems and start serving to our own purpose. S.T.O.P.'s new meaning can be Serving To our Own Purpose. You can turn your stories of pain into stories of peace. Forgive yourself for your own mistakes. The only true way of feeling valuable enough of forgiveness is to let go completely of the need to be perfect.

As you will read, I have found too many similarities with those who suffer from anxiety. The specific issues are different, but the perfectionism, the pain of the past, the procrastination, and the people pleasing are usually a constant. (I call these the 4 P's.) My goal of this book is that you will learn through my example and many stories how to change the stories of your past that are plaguing you. I hope you will learn here how to change your reaction to your past to create your very best present and future self. It is all in how you see your stories and how you have learned the lessons. If your stories are not working for you, change them. See them differently. I can teach you how.

It is important to me that readers of this book understand from the beginning some assumptions of mine. These are some baseline beliefs of mine that I hope you will take into account:

1. I do not believe in coincidences. "It" had to happen that way; it was meant to happen that way. Now learn the lessons.

2. I believe everything happens for a good reason. We might not ever fully understand the reasons, but it was for your good. Again, learn the lessons.

3. The greater the pain in life, the greater is the opportunity to grow immensely. It should not be, "No pain, no gain," but instead, "More pain, more chance for growth." The growth though is not an automatic with pain. With greater pain, you are given the OPPORTUNITY to grow only if (you guessed it) you learn the lessons.

4. I believe that God gave us a packet of lessons to learn in this life AND the gifts to learn those lessons. We have been given the ingredients to grow, but we have to do our part. The key here is to spend time and energy learning our own, individual, personalized lessons, not others' lessons.

5. I think there are only a certain number of lessons to learn in life. If a previous generation did not learn the lessons, the lessons get passed onto another generation. If you lack incentive to change for you alone, do it for your children or for future generations. History will continue to repeat itself until the lessons have fully been learned.

6. In order to fully grow, at some point in life every individual needs to stop playing the blame game. It has been your choice to continue to define yourself by what has happened to you in the past. It is no longer helpful to find fault with others for your problems. This book can greatly help you to get released from the prison walls of the past, but this process will only work if you accept full responsibility for how you have processed the meaning of your past. Remember belief #1. It had to happen that way in order for you to learn the greatest lesson. Your prison can become your greatest freedom.

7. The lessons God gives you have a lot to do with what has happened in your generational line in the past. We cannot focus on learning the lessons from past generations though because our

lessons have been individualized for us alone. Maybe we all are serving others' penance for those who came before us.

Those are many of my baseline beliefs at the time of writing this book. I am still discovering and growing. I know these beliefs will evolve down the road, but I hope they provide you with peace of mind. Safe travels on your roads of discovery!

Chapter Seven: Memories

"If you think nobody cares about you, try missing a couple of payments."
— Steven Wright

From as early back as being a little girl, I remember my grandfather telling me a story of when he was in school. He was telling me how mean his teachers were. One of his classmates once was leaning back in his chair, and the teacher threw a piece of chalk at him to get him to stop doing it. Instead of the teacher getting into trouble for throwing the chalk, the student had to report to the principal's office. The student was in trouble, not the teacher. I heard that story repeatedly over the years.

Unfortunately, I kind of tune out when I hear the same stories over and over again. However, one time I was really listening and heard him tell this childhood story a little differently. This time, he said that when the teacher threw the chalk, the student fell backwards on his chair and got seriously hurt.

Fast forward many years later, and as I sat with my Poppa in the hallway of his nursing home, he told the story again. This time, the student fell back, hit his head, and died. "No, wait, what, Poppa? What happened to the student? Did you say he died? I thought he only got seriously hurt." My Poppa was absolutely convinced that his friend had died. Despite the fact that my Poppa had experienced a number of strokes, his memory of the end of that story was as real to my Poppa as I was sitting right there.

Memories in general are elastic. You do not have to have suffered any brain trauma in order for your memories to change. Once you understand the elasticity/adaptability of memories, you know that the actual facts of what happened in history are not as important as the reactions to those facts.

Rorschach's psychological tests have at their foundation the idea that people see pictures differently. It does not seem that far of a stretch to say that people recall events differently. My friend and I went to school together from kindergarten through college, and we roomed together for three of the four college years. We experienced so many of the actual events, but our impressions are drastically different. That is mostly due to our vision of those events being seen through vastly different lenses. It still fascinates me when I hear her memory of events as she sees them because so many times it is as if we were at completely different functions.

Now, get this. When we get together, we go over the same events as we had done the last get together. The way I tell the story of one event is different even from the way I told it a few years ago. I emphasize new things, remember new parts of the story, and maybe see the event more positively as time advances. I am different now from the last time I told the stories. My memories are different from my friend's but also from the me of my past. Memories change.

Have you ever left a meeting with a colleague, and as you are discussing what happened, you start scratching your head wondering if you were in the same meeting as your colleague? I mean, you saw them in the meeting, but the way they are describing the meeting feels like an entirely different meeting. They heard what they wanted to hear as much as you heard what you wanted to hear. If you had been in an argument with your boss right before the meeting, your vision of your boss' demeanor at that meeting was probably entirely different from how your colleague saw your boss. How about siblings' views of childhood? There is a twelve-year age gap between my brother and me. When we talk about our childhoods, we have completely different impressions even though we grew up in the same family.

Why is the elasticity of memories important? It is important to know what is changing. The facts of a memory are not changing. Our focus and personal reaction to the memories can be changed though. We can change our emotional investment into the memory. This is key to personal growth, especially for anyone who has suffered from their past.

The locus of control is all within you. No longer does the destruction of your prison walls depend on anyone else! If you suffered abuse as a child, you could change your emotional reaction to that past. You do not have to depend on the abuser to help you. Of course, it is not as easy as I just said it, but most people feel there is no way out of changing what happened to them.

I am living proof that you can change something that has been bothering you for years. One problem's resolution took me almost thirty years, but my strong, emotional reaction is gone. This issue still needs some healing at times, and I need to perform some wellness checks to make sure that I have not lapsed into some old thought patterns, but it is no longer affecting my current problems. Please don't think your resolution will take thirty years. I found some major shortcuts and am helping people every day with changing the stories of their past. You can release yourself from your prison's walls.

I have studied financial guru Dave Ramsey for many, many years. I learned about him while flipping the dial on the radio and came across Dave's program as he was telling us the Scripture of the day. I was hooked for Dave relating Scripture with financial responsibility. That was my kind of music on the radio. I am now proud to say I am a Dave Ramsey Master Financial Coach. Bottom line is I have studied his teachings a lot. At one presentation, he was relating how hard it is for him to hear people making excuses. As Dave was telling an employee who was reluctant to change the current behavior, Dave just said how easy it was and to watch what can be done. Dave clapped his hands twice while saying, "Change." It is not magic. You do have to first decide to act and to stop making excuses or placing blame. Decide to change.

I really don't think Dave was being flippant with clapping twice. He is the first one to admit the major mistakes he has made. He says that he has a PhD in D.U.M.B. It is not easy to change, but first the decision has to be made to change. Once Dorothy clicked her heels twice, she was ready for her path, but she still had a long journey to Oz.

If there is a past memory that is not working for you, that is holding you back, and that you can't seem to forget, are you doomed to being burdened by its heavy weight for the rest of your life? No. Clap twice, and decide you are going to change how you feel about that memory. Begin by deciding that you are in control to change it.

Chapter Eight: Don't Push the Trigger

I am a really safe driver. My family likes to joke that if I were to get a speeding ticket, it would probably be for going too slowly. However, I started to notice that my personality completely changed when someone would cut me off in traffic. This angst had been happening for years, but one day I was cut off for the last time, and I forced myself to look at my reaction.

I remember the exact place on the road when a driver completely cut me off by turning left right in front of me. After breaking hard to avoid hitting him, I next looked in my rear-view mirror. There was not a car in sight. The aggressive driver only had to wait milliseconds for me to pass but instead chose to cut me off and risked it all to save milliseconds. I was so happy just seconds earlier, but after seeing no car behind me, I turned instantaneously into a candidate for mandated, anger management therapy. I forced myself to look at such a dramatic reaction and my immediate personality transformation.

The driver acted as if I did not exist. Wait a minute. Say that last part again - like I did not exist. Like Dory having a vague memory of having been warned where not to swim, I had a vague memory of pain from not being recognized. There was a painful memory of people acting like I did not exist. As soon as I said that in my mind, I flashed back to a fancy airport lounge on our way to an exciting land. My Dad had just commented about me having pierced ears. I was in my early twenties at the time. "Hey, Ead, you have pierced ears." Though I managed to answer with a simple, "Yes, Dad, I do," I was absolutely crushed. I had pierced my ears when I was sixteen years old, and my Dad just noticed now. I realized at that moment that my father rarely looked at me. It was as if I did not exist in his mind. This airport memory was just one example of a childhood of being opaque.

I finally pieced the connection together. Being cut off in traffic resembled being cut off from my father's life. I understand how silly it sounds to others, but for the next several times I was cut off in traffic after having made the connection, I repeated to myself, "I exist. I exist. They are just selfish." Little by little, I started to feel less and less of an emotional reaction to being cut off in traffic. Now when I drive, I am just focused on the safety of all and there not being an accident.

My reaction to being cut off, my friend, was a trigger. It triggered some unresolved pain from my past. I ignored the signals for years, but after finally confronting this immediate change of personality, the cure was relatively easy to implement.

When do you feel triggered? What emotional reactions have you been putting off reviewing? While triggers are painful, they are also windows into the meaning you have placed on something in your past. This book is here to give you reasons to look at your current problems in light of where you have been. Have you ever worked on a problem and felt you were tackling the solution in the wrong way? Unless we peel back the layers of the problem, we cannot get the best resolution. If I had not been willing "to go there," I probably never would have fully seen the reason I felt so badly emotionally when cut off in traffic.

This example of connecting my anger while driving and my father's rejection set me on a path of taking a deeper look at many current problems. Basically, it comes down to everything is connected. When you look at your own problems, try to connect the dots to similar negative feelings from your past.

I have to point out something about triggers though in terms of your responsibility. Recently, I have watched some real-life examples of people being triggered. These people are irate at others calling them particular names that trigger their unresolved pasts. While it is not okay to call people names and purposely trigger anger, it also is one's own responsibility to handle their triggers. Instead of seeing triggers as danger signs to avoid, we can see them as windows of opportunity to change our reactions. Triggers are really lessons that need to be learned.

Use this book as a journey to find the connection of that problem to your past. Who you are today has everything to do with where you have journeyed already. Very technically, your past is anything that has happened to you earlier. For the purposes of this book, I would like to focus on the past that is probably most affecting how you were shaped - your childhood. Again, very technically, your childhood is any time before eighteen years of age. But, earlier childhood years are more formative, more dependent on others' opinions, views, teachings, and most importantly the labels you were given.

I cannot tell you how many clients ultimately reveal their guilt on not doing more for a loved one. Unless you have known the guilt of feeling responsible for another's pain, it is difficult to describe how hard it is to gain traction falling down the hole. The retelling of the story to learn how to protect yourself and others is agonizing. It is almost like I attract people who cannot breathe from their own guilt. By helping to release them from the way they have convicted themselves, I am able to release myself more of the past's chains. The way I processed life was all of my own problem. It's our own mind's court, judge, jury, and prosecution that get in the way sometimes. You can appeal your own sentence. Use this book to retell your story that honors your goodness.

Find your own triggers. Think of this book as an opportunity to be your own Agatha Christie or Sherlock Holmes to the mysteries of your pain.

Chapter Nine: Put the Label Maker Down!

This is a physical label maker. Actual label makers are the only label makers we should be using in life, but we unfortunately usually carry a mental label maker with us. The reality is that we have been given a lot of labels in our lifetime, especially at childhood, that we felt we had no other option than to accept. The labels from childhood that parents or others have given us feel like permanent labels. Do you wear the label of "not a good student?" Do you still wear labels of lazy, selfish, uncoordinated, or stupid? I try to catch people whenever I hear them saying their negative, childhood labels out loud, but if I pointed out every instance, the process would completely envelope my day. It might sound silly, but it especially bugs me when I hear people say they are not a math person. Math might not be your thing, but by continuing to label yourself as not good at math, the simplest of math problems becomes daunting.

It is critical to increase your awareness of your labels from the past, especially childhood. You've lived with others' labels for a long time, and it has been so long that now these labels have moved to your subconscious. You aren't even aware of the extent of the negativity of your self-talk after years and years of playing the broken record in your mind. Start listening to your self-talk. Your words spoken out loud though are worse than your mental self-talk because you are using even more of your senses when you are saying the negative labels out loud. If you continue to speak your negative labels out loud, you are cementing them into your mind and into the mind of others.

I have a friend who I considered highly organized. I still think she is a fabulous Mom, but I have heard her say so many times how disorganized her house is that I only see disorganization now when I visit. She convinced me that my positive label of organized was not true. Notice here though that her house and the arrangement of the items didn't change. How I saw those items went from organized to disorganized all based on her words. It was almost as if my actual vision of her home became irrelevant.

I could never be a medical doctor or a nurse. But, if I had to describe my work in the medical profession, the closest I could come would be to describe myself is an eye specialist because I work on others' vision problems. Your labels given to you in your past by others or self-imposed might be affecting how you can resolve the problems in your present time. Your own labels of how you processed the meaning of your past are likely holding you up from living your best life.

It is time to put the label maker down. When we are children, we rely on our family to tell us who we are. But, when we become adults, we have to test those labels to see if the given labels are truly who we are or if they are who others want us to be. As an adult now, by making new labels that work, you no longer have to be limited by your past. This book is not about living in the past, but an unreconciled past owns you. You can create new labels that honor how to use your God-given gifts to be your best self. After reading this book, you will be able to reconstruct the stories of your past so that they are working FOR you and not against you.

Chapter Ten: Expert

"I went to France. Let me give you a heads up. Chapeau means hat; oeuf means egg. It's like they have a different word for everything."
— Steve Martin

I don't even want to know how much time, money, work, and energy I have invested into the initials past my name. I am state mandated to complete countless hours of continuing education every year for my two licenses. I take numerous certifications, attend countless classes, have transformed my car's stereo into my audible university, and read extensively about personal development. With all of that, what prepared me most to be the expert to write this book is my personal relationship with anxiety and my thirty-year journey to master my mind's stories. I have the technical expertise through both education and experience to treat those who suffer from anxiety, but I also bring a judgment-free zone because I really understand what it is like.

I am a licensed counselor and have a certification in Cognitive Behavioral Therapy (CBT). CBT is one of the best tools to combat anxiety. I market my counseling services as serving anxiety issues. However, the reality is that I feel my best qualifications are that I have lived with many different types of anxiety from an early age. As I have learned to heal myself of one form, another form tests me. The dream of this book is that your real demons from any kind of anxiety will be better understood from my journey. Travel with me.

When you have cancer, you seek an experienced oncologist. One of the many requirements you would seek in a good doctor would probably not be that they have survived cancer. However, an oncologist who has had cancer would probably treat their patients with much more compassion and heart. That doctor would be able to see how important mental attitude, fortitude, positivity, and hope are in the treatment plan.

Other than Alcoholics Anonymous or any other twelve step program, treatment plans are not administered by people with that disorder. Those with severe mental health disorders are usually not treating others with the same disorders, and I really don't think it would be a good idea to start either. However, my hypothesis is that licensed therapists who have suffered and also who have "mastered" anxiety are some of the best helpers to anxiety sufferers.

When you are training to be a therapist, you learn about a concept called countertransference. Transference is when clients/patients unconsciously transfer some of their feelings or issues onto therapists. Countertransference then is when therapists transfer or at least recognize similar feelings from their own lives in the therapy work. When I say that someone with anxiety might be the best person to help another with anxiety, countertransference issues should not be involved. A therapist needs to be keenly aware of their own triggers and well versed in taking self-care measures. They must have really dealt with and healed their own anxiety to a point where they can help others. Even though you will learn that this is a constant process of self-care, a therapist should have done their own personal homework on mastering their mind. Whatever their own cure was, therapists really need to feel they have put anxiety in its proper place. Self-care is a continuous must, but by handling one's own anxiety of the past, a therapist can really be the best of teachers.

Obsessive Compulsive Disorder (OCD), hoarding, panic attacks, and even math phobia are different types of anxiety disorders. There are a lot of different types of anxiety with important differences. There is not one typical type who suffers from anxiety, but a large group of sufferers are highly intelligent, highly successful professionals in their own fields. When someone who is so highly functional tries to explain that they have trouble going outside because of social anxiety, most people just don't understand it, including therapists. There is such a shame component in trying to explain a shortcoming, and unless you have been through it, it is hard to understand why some cannot open and exit the door to their own homes.

I once worked as a business manager for a staff of less than one hundred people. I went to my mail slot one day, and the slot was completely jam packed with flyers announcing a workshop. The slot was so full I couldn't even manage to get the flyers out of it without a lot of effort. At the top of my mail slot was a paper with a down arrow, indicating I had additional mail in a box on the floor. That large box had numerous copies of the same flyer. I took all of the flyers to my office and turned over the flyer to read the topic. Then, I looked for the Candid Cameras watching me. The title of the workshop was, "How to Eliminate the Paper in Your Office." I had about three times the number of flyers than the number of employees of the whole organization. They had chosen not to send an email communication but wasted all of that paper instead. They did not research how many copies our company might need. My next task was that I threw all of the flyers in the trash. Workshop was over. I also saw an advertisement that read, "Seventy-Five Time Management Strategies." Seventy-five? Stop reading the tips, and you just saved yourself a lot of time. These "experts" were anything but experts. Let's make sure we are surrounding ourselves with true experts in their fields.

If you have been through an experience and have seen the other side, you could help people get there too. You are an expert in conquering the demons in your own world. I was at a convention once where a top saleswoman was teaching us why we have an obligation to serve where we are experts. As a Mom of five, she learned (the hard way) a technique to get a fussy baby to sleep. She said it worked - Every. Single. Time. Let's say this Mom creates a program to teach this technique and decides to sell it. If this entrepreneur sees a mother stressed out and sleep deprived because the baby is not sleeping, wouldn't it be wrong to withhold this technique from this poor woman because she was charging for the tips? What if the expert does not want to come off as pushy or "salesy" and withholds the product, was the customer served? If you have mastered something, why is it wrong to profit from teaching others how to benefit too?

I have been less than five miles from my home but unable to get home because I just kept driving around the block in fear I hit someone. When we cleaned out a relative's home after they died, there were thousands of plastic bags hidden all over their home. I work with many people who feel they truly are not enough. Many people I know are consumed with what others think of them.

It just can't be a coincidence that people suffer with the same kind of issues. Plastic bags are quite common to hoard. Many are plagued with worry that they've hit someone or something. I just think there has to be a connection where so many feel exactly the same thing. Anxiety is not like a physical disorder where you can look it up on Webmd.com to find, "The next symptom is driving around the same block in fear you've hit someone." Yet, people with anxiety seem to suffer from remarkably similar symptoms. I'm here to try to point out those similarities and to teach what has worked for me and for many others.

If you have a plumbing emergency where an expert arrives at night and solves the problem in less than a half hour, do you feel you should be charged less because it didn't take them long? The repair took them less than thirty minutes, but learning how to repair the solution took ten years of experience. The issue of one's value comes up all the time in my accounting world. The services I perform for my clients are so much more than bookkeeping, and my clients completely recognize the value of peace of mind giving me their financial information. However, my Facebook accounting group members are endlessly complaining about having to justify to potential clients their value. This is just a reality. The problem arises when we start questioning our own value.

Find the areas where you are doubting your value. As you read this book, consider how you have processed the experiences of your past, how you've incorporated others' labels, and what needs changing. Part One of this book has been about the connection of the stories of our past to our current problems. Part Two is a collection of a few stories that have helped shape me to write this book. I hope you learn how to be exceptionally good at showing yourself grace and self-forgiveness.

Part II: People Pleasers Anonymous

I am on a mission to give people a blueprint to the past to cure their own present anxiety. The starting point is recognizing the stories of the past and how you have processed the meaning of life from those stories. I feel a strong connection to others who have suffered from self-imposed limitations. I think there is a formula to diagnose anxiety, and I am out to prove there is a formula for its mastery too.

Hop on my bus, Gus. I have personally traveled this road, and I know the path to freedom. You can learn how to stop serving penance and start serving to your own, unique purpose. If you struggle to be your truest self, learn from my path of self-discovery.

Let me tell you a story…

Chapter Eleven: Bricks

The doctor was a real piece of work. It really was quite a talent to be able to clear a room just at the sound of your heels clicking down the hallway. She was a doctor with issues, big issues. Self-awareness was not one of her talents; all her issues quickly became others' hell.

I had heard so many stories of her outrageous antics. Nurses would tell me story after story of how she crushed person after person because they did not do their job with the exact precision that she demanded. She was a neurosurgeon. No one could joke that it was not brain surgery because it was! With her, everything needed to be as precise and as perfect as her brain surgeries had to be. She never turned it off.

No one goes to a hospital to see a social worker. Labeled discharge planners, social workers are low ones on the totem pole, the first feed for wild beasts. Once the hospital personnel where I worked discovered a patient on my floor had a grenade, and they sent me in to check it out! Even with my low status, I still had not suffered at the hands of this perfect neurologist. As a social worker specializing in stroke patients and their families, contact with neurologists was a common event for me. I was tempting fate, but so far, I had not suffered her sting.

My office/closet on the medical floor was just behind the nurses' station. One day, I emerged to put the patient files back in the slots. As I turned the corner, no one was there. "Where is everybody?" I innocently asked. Then, I heard it. It was very faint at first, and then the rattling of her high heels was deafening. The nurses had scattered into their patients' rooms. The nurses left me alone to be put in front of Dr. D's firing squad. Thanks, guys. Just as I realized I had no time to escape, our eyes met. Have you ever seen Mogli look into the snake's eyes in The Jungle Book? I had no chance.

However, in this case, I gave her extra feed for fodder. I had been instructed by my supervisors to put a note in patients' files if we thought they qualified for the physical rehabilitation unit. How did I know they qualified if I was not a doctor? Basically, if they had a stroke, a small note to remind the main physician that our hospital had a stroke rehabilitation unit might drum up business.

That is not exactly how Dr. D saw it. She felt I was playing doctor. I do not think I had ever been tarred and feathered before on my actions. There are PLENTY of times I have subjected myself to my own, critical firing squad of shame, but rarely did others feel the need to add to my own self-judgmental punishments. I do not remember a lot during or immediately after the public shaming, but I can recall seeing the small note I had in the file put within inches of my face, being ripped to shreds. In this bizarre way though, I felt nothing. Though the self-proclaimed Queen of Guilt, I actually had zero remorse. I had only done what I had been instructed to do by my supervisors. I was not owning the problem at all. (That must have been apparent to the doctor too because that was driving her crazy.) Or, at least I thought then it was not bothering me.

It was a beautiful Saturday morning, and my husband (boyfriend at that time) and I drove to Dr. D's home. While it looked like a modest home, I later found out it was a two-story mansion. Dr. D greeted us at the door, with about as much enthusiasm as she does when seeing a social worker at the hospital. She walked us down the hallway and opened a bedroom door on the first floor. The floor was covered from floor to ceiling with bricks.

"Your job is to take each brick and to bring them upstairs to the first bedroom at the top of the stairs."

OK, let's get cracking. That was it. The instructions were very clear. How we were responsible for her home repairs wasn't clear, but there wasn't a question in my mind of what needed to be done. There also was no question in my husband's mind; that was an interesting observation about our future together. Have you ever tried to lift bricks? How many do you think you can hold and still climb a full flight of stairs? My husband was able to lift more than what I could, but I was holding up my end of the arrangement and doing a fairly good job. Was Dr. D helping us? What do you think? We were not able to enjoy the beautiful Saturday outside. I can't recall if there was air conditioning, but I just remember being physically taxed, overheated, and drained.

After many, many hours of hard, physical labor, we had completed the task. The upstairs bedroom, that exactly resembled one of my high school classrooms by the way, was larger than the downstairs bedroom. Therefore, the bricks didn't cover the entire floor to ceiling, but the enormity of the number of bricks we had lifted still looked daunting. Ah, the satisfaction of a completed job was a new thing for me. I am an excellent project starter, but the finishing... (See? I didn't even finish that last sentence.)

Do you think Dr. D praised us? Again, what do you think? The three of us stood looking at the bricks for a long moment of silence. I don't know what two of us were thinking, but I knew what I was thinking and better yet what I was feeling. I was confused, tired, and angry.

After quite some time of awkward silence, Dr. D announced, "OK, now. I need you to take these bricks and to bring them back down to the downstairs bedroom."

"Where we just were?"
"Yes."

45

Wait. What? We have to bring the bricks that we already brought upstairs back downstairs? The absurdity of carrying the first load was now being topped by an even crazier scheme to have us go insane. Did we hesitate? Did we argue with the mean doctor? My husband merely picked up the first three bricks that were closest to him. I reached down for one that was next to me and then stood up quickly.

"Wait a minute. THESE ARE NOT MY BRICKS!"

Bam! Pow! At that very moment, I woke up. I still remember that dream after almost thirty years. But, I even more clearly remember the lesson. I tended to carry other people's bricks, and evidently so did my husband. I will put myself through back-breaking work without even a thought if someone EXPECTS me to deliver for them. To what lengths will I go?

Lesson Learned: Carry Only My Own Bricks

Ever since that dream, I have the opportunity to frequently ask myself if I am carrying my bricks or someone else's. The objective lacked any purpose; it didn't seem to help even Dr. D. It was a futile exercise. This too has served an important reminder for me to serve in my capacity, when it is purposeful, and when the bricks are mine.

Of course, this does not mean that I can't help others even if they are not my bricks. If I feel I can be of service to someone with my gifts and talents, if it will really help them, if they cannot do it for themselves, and if there is a purpose that is ethical and improves their situation, there really is no reason why I wouldn't want to help someone.

I carry a lot of bricks that have nothing to do with me. Why? I'm not sure, but I have a few guesses. Also, my husband is so loving that if I haven't questioned the task at hand, he won't either. He was the first one in my dream to pick up the bricks the second time around to a place where we started. It was back-breaking work with zero purpose, and yet there we were serving someone else's penance. If the Good Lord wanted me to carry bricks, He would have given me a stronger back. There is a purpose for my life that has to do with my own work. When I exit the bus at the pearly gates of Heaven (more on that with CS Lewis), I really think I will be judged by the way I used my gifts and how I served my purposes. Did I turn my talents into double the investment for my Master, or did I serve someone else's plans? Am I so distracted with pleasing others that I am blind to my own mission? Is God pleased?

When do you carry others' bricks?

What are your bricks?

When do you find yourself in people pleasing mode usually? What groups of people are you usually trying to please? Is there a pattern? (Please don't be ashamed to write down that you please total strangers or people that drive you nuts. That is quite common.) How do you know when others are pleased? Usually, we have constructed a full and complete story of what we THINK others are expecting. Most of the time, we do not even check that thought against the reality of expectations. We aim to please what we think others expect in order for us to feel good about ourselves. And, said in a Dr. Phil voice, how is that working out for you? When will enough be enough?

Chapter Twelve: Rock the Mind's Boat!

My husband and I met at casino night in a nursing home. When his friends found out he had a girlfriend, they asked him, "Hey, Gardner, where do you meet girls?" "Oh, just go to your local nursing home." My husband and I dated for EIGHT YEARS before we got married. By the time I was walking down the aisle, we knew that we were meant for each other. I knew from the core of my soul that God wanted us to be together. And, yet… something happened on our honeymoon that made me think that maybe there was an issue.

We decided to splurge on our honeymoon by going to Tahiti. Even though we are the poster children for sunscreen, we both love tropical islands. I do not swim in oceans, and my husband is bald. But, yet, there is some draw deep within both of us to be near an ocean.

We were having a magical time. Our original hotel on the island of Bora Bora had suffered tremendous damage from a previous hurricane, and we were put up in a five star hotel. The regular rooms were full, and at check in, they asked if we were okay staying in the honeymoon suite which was really the honeymoon apartment on the beach. "Yes, if that's all there is, it will have to do." Pierce Brosnan had just stayed in that very same, heavenly oasis. It was surreal.

At the end of our amazing honeymoon, we had a few days to explore the capital of Tahiti, Pape'ete. We had explored the main city and wanted to finish the day by walking down the street to get a drink at a nearby hotel also on the beach. As we entered the bar, it was jam packed with people for a bachelor party. There were a few couches in a corner with an open couch for us. As we were enjoying the sunset, a couple came over and asked to sit with us.

They introduced themselves as did we, and they were amused that we were there on our honeymoon. The man was significantly older than the woman, and at first I wondered if she was his daughter. I asked why they were here, and the woman said that they were waiting for a piece for their boat to arrive. They explained that they were sailing around the world, and their boat had broken in Tahiti. It was a rare part, and they were waiting for it to arrive. I was absolutely fascinated that they had no place (other than the boat) to call home. "How did you get your mail," was the first of many questions that I had. I really wanted to know how they made money, but I was not brave enough to ask that. Oh, and yeah, they were definitely not father and daughter. Why, why, why did I have to be so fascinated with their carefree life because I am afraid my curiosity set things off.

"Why don't you come out on our boat tomorrow to see for yourself?"

"Oh, no, we couldn't." That is my code for I absolutely do not want to do that. They did not speak my language.

"Yes, really, please come. How about 1:00 right here?"

We downed the rest of our drinks and quickly headed out of there. On the walk back to our hotel, my husband innocently said, "So, I guess we have plans at 1:00 tomorrow."

"What? No, we don't have to go." I do not even know who this person was who said this because what I meant was that I knew we were obligated to do something we desperately did not want to do.

"We told them we would."

"But, we don't even know them."

"Still, we have to go."

"Did it seem kind of weird that they are mysteriously waiting for a boat part? Where is the part going to be sent? They are not staying at the hotel and do not have an address. I think they need money for that boat part and are waiting to get money. Do you think they are going to ask us for money?"

"Uh-oh."

"We don't have anything left from splurging on our honeymoon. We can't give them any money."

"Ok, if we feel really pressured, what is our limit that we'll give them."

"WE DON'T HAVE ANY MONEY TO GIVE THEM."

"What if they don't accept that as an answer. We'll be on their boat without any way to escape."

That was just the conversation to our hotel. By the time we actually got into bed, we had concocted a story that if we did not give them ALL of our non-existent money, they were going to kill us. Actually, even if we gave them some money, they were still likely to kill us. That was when we went to bed, but of course neither of us got any sleep that night.

By morning, the story had progressed to us being poisoned through tasty, fruity drinks. They would threaten to kill one of us if the other one did not give them everything.

Here comes the fun part. All we had to do was not show up at the hotel bar at 1:00. On some level, I am sure we knew that, but after all, we were people pleasers.

WHAT WOULD THEY THINK OF US IF WE DIDN'T SHOW?

Yes, that type of thinking is the stinkin' thinkin' that gets us all in trouble. We were so sleep deprived that we were convinced they were going to kill us. We were so convinced that we even left a note in the safe that read, "If we never show up at our rooms again, we went on a boat owned by a couple we met at the hotel next door. This is the name of their boat and their first names. Please call Edie's mother at this number. We most likely have been kidnapped and probably killed."

I don't know what it is like to walk the plank, but in a way, I kind of do know. Our only plan was that they couldn't poison us if we didn't take the drinks. Our rule was the only drink we would drink would be a soda from an unopened can. That was such a wonderful plan. What could go wrong?

"In death do us part" never seemed more real than then. All one of us had to do was announce, "Wait a minute. What are we doing? We don't have to go somewhere with total strangers just because we don't want them to think we think they are weird."

I kid you not, but the first thing out of the woman's mouth when she saw us on the beach was, "Oh, wow. I didn't think you guys were going to show up."

See? That WAS an option. Even the kidnapper/murderer didn't believe anyone could be so foolish as to go to a stranger's boat.

We went in their Zodiac a long way out to sea to board their boat. Remember our plan was to just not drink anything unless it was in a soda can. Exiting the Zodiac was difficult to balance, and so the woman helped my husband board their ladder first. The man then had me go up the ladder. On my first step off the Zodiac and onto the ladder, I hear the woman offer my husband a drink they had pre-made and had put in a small watermelon. Remember the plan, hubby. Only soda cans for drinks. Stay strong.

"Sure, if you went to all that trouble." Great, he's dead.

Fast forward. They served us tasty, fruity drinks. We had stimulating conversation. They never asked us for money. We made it safely back to shore. We were alive.

Was it the wisest thing to do? Of course, there wasn't one wise thought or move in this whole scenario. However, even when we felt our lives were at stake, we felt the need to please people trumped even our own safety. I wholeheartedly believe that life should always be protected. But, this was people pleasing on steroids. We both couldn't stand the idea that they would make the effort to go back to the beach and not find us there.

Would it be the worst thing in the world for strangers to see us as flaky or selfish? Of course, it doesn't seem even remotely bad right now, but it really did then. This incident was when I realized my husband and I will need to forever keep our people pleasing efforts at bay. Even when the price is our own safety, we place great value in people pleasing.

If you are absolutely convinced you are a good person with good intentions, people pleasing becomes less and less an issue. There isn't a need for it. If we had strong convictions of our own value, it would have been much easier to allow ourselves to say no, thank you to the couple. If we prioritized our value, we would have focused more on what was in our control. It was possible to say no, remain polite, feel safe, and not worry at POSSIBLY disappointing someone. Whatever they thought about us was beyond our control. Whatever anyone thinks about us is ultimately out of our control. Wouldn't it be better to focus our energies into areas that are under our control?

When I am working with someone who suffers from anxiety, it usually becomes apparent early on in our work that there are self-confidence and/or self-worth issues. If we work ridiculously hard to please someone to have them think of us a certain way, that usually indicates we have doubts that we really are a particular way. As Dr. Phil says, "How is that working out for you?" Pleasing people is a game that is never won.

The other huge lesson for me here was how much our own thoughts can run amuck. It didn't take long for us to imagine they were going to ask us for money, jumping then to them poisoning us. Our minds can find creative ways to play tricks on us. Plus, these were conscious thoughts. Working with anxiety is a process of uncovering the unconscious thoughts that have become broken records in our minds. We aren't even aware of these thoughts because they are such hard-wired habits. This is where talk therapy and journaling are quite helpful to finding the unconscious thoughts that are working behind the scenes.

If you suffer from anxiety, odds are that you are a people pleaser. In what social situations do you find yourself people pleasing the most?

Where do you feel you fall short and cannot show your truest self?

Chapter Thirteen: The Great Divorce

I am immensely proud to tell you that I am a devout Catholic. My faith in God is everything to me, and it is important for me to tell the reader my focus up front. Therefore, it might seem odd to you that a devout Catholic should title a chapter with two seemingly contradictory words in the title. How can a Roman Catholic think that a divorce can in any way be great? *The Great Divorce* is the title of one of my most favorite books of all time.

Thank goodness I was there at that Mass at that time on that day. I do not think I ever would have read the book if not for the priest's homily that day, opening up my world to CS Lewis. The priest was a student of everything that had to do with CS Lewis, and this life-long study meant that the churchgoers that day were going to be given a lifetime gift. C.S. Lewis' book *The Great Divorce* depicts the predicaments of many passengers on a bus route to (and from) the gates before Heaven and the passengers' ability or inability to let go. Of what should they let go, you ask? It is anything that prevents them from getting to Heaven. Some passengers are addicted to things, others are addicted to other people, and still others are confined to looking at life in their own way, stuck in their ways. Some passengers are able to divorce themselves from their dependencies; others know the gates to Heaven are so close but just cannot divorce themselves from what they know and seemingly love the most.

The priest went on to explain that we are all given opportunities to let go of what we cling to the most in life. In order to get off the bus and enter Heaven, we have to give up what we think we love the most. I just said above that my faith is everything, but am I strong enough in my faith to give up everything else I love to God? Could I sacrifice as much as Abraham was willing to sacrifice? I would love to think so, but I am just not sure. But, as I journeyed through the book and the bus route to and from Heaven with CS Lewis, I learned so many examples of how what we cling to might not always be leading us to Heaven but also might not be contributing to our happiness here on earth.

There are lots of contradictions and ironies in life. We love things that are not good for us. We do things to our bodies that feel good at the moment but shorten our lives. We are given the garden of Eden with only one tree to avoid, and yet, the one thing we cannot have is what we want the most.

Thanks to CS Lewis, I see now that all of life is a continuous bus route. The bus picks up passengers at each bus stop of life and takes them to the gates of Heaven. When the lessons to let go are not learned, the passengers return back onto the bus. What if we are just living out our lives as one part of the bus stop?

What if we are carrying the luggage from our ancestors' previous bus trips who were unable to let go of their baggage to reach Heaven?

This is how I think life goes. Before we are born into this world, we are given a book of lessons and a toolbox to help learn those lessons. We hop onto the bus. Our job is to learn those lessons. These lessons have been passed down from other bus passengers throughout history who were not able to learn the full lessons in their lives. If we do not learn our own lessons, they get passed down farther to other bus riders. Every time though that we learn a lesson fully, we pick up former riders who had to get off the bus earlier.

We are all connected. Now, we can and should help others to learn their lessons. We can help them onto the bus. By helping others, we are advancing our own lesson plans too. However, and this is oh so important, we cannot learn other people's lessons. We help them onto the bus, but we cannot ride the bus for them. It is not our responsibility to ride the bus for them.

In Catholicism, we learn it as Heaven, Purgatory, and Hell. Purgatory is that "place" where souls go who have passed from this life but who are not ready to reach Heaven. We pray for those in Purgatory. I am just defining our prayers to have more action. By learning our own life lessons, we are helping those in Purgatory to get closer to Heaven. We are their second and third and so on chances. We cannot learn the lessons they were supposed to learn, but we get glimpses into their lessons through our DNA.

Our chemical makeup in our DNA is just one window into what others before us were supposed to have learned. Those who did not learn to take care of themselves might have passed down addictions and struggles for others to overcome. For example, I have had a cough all of my life but have never smoked. Many think I am a smoker by my cough. Do I suffer from a severe cough because someone in my genealogy could not master taking care of themselves? On a more positive note, I have been blessed with an absolute love of needlework. Anything that involves sewing or crafting, I am all in. My ancestry on both sides of my family is rich with sewers and crafters. Your genes carry much more than high/low cholesterol, high/low BP, or histories of diseases.

Role modeling the values you want to instill is the way to make sure you have done all you can to equip your children with the tools for a happy life. Your children might not take those tools on their road of life, but you will have provided the tools. Remember you get a lesson book and a toolbox. That toolbox is rich with tools from your ancestry.

In the Disney movie Finding Nemo, Dory is a fish friend who has short-term memory problems. She knows things but cannot remember why she knows some things. Haven't we all had a feeling that we know something to be true, but we do not know how we know it? Does a proven fact make it any less valid if you cannot remember why you know it? If you have a natural talent singing, calculating math equations, or playing baseball but have not had formal training, are you any less talented? If you have lived a long time, there are plenty of situations where you have developed a gut instinct, but you cannot specifically identify the source of that knowledge. Maybe in life our "memories" are not limited to our lifetimes, but our memories are enhanced by the knowledge from our ancestors.

So maybe our knowledge, our loves, and our pain come partially from our ancestors. Then, we pass onto the next generations more knowledge and more unlearned lessons of our inability to let go of that to which we cling. Can we divorce ourselves in this life to something that is great to gain something that is the GREATEST?

On what or on whom do you depend the most?

Why?

What frightens you on giving up where you depend the most?

Chapter Fourteen: The Cough

The comedian, Gallagher would frequently call out to someone coughing in the audience. "Do you smoke?"

"No!"

"Well, you ought to. You've already got the cough."

"Edie, if you want to date in college, don't cough." Those were the last words my brother told me as I headed off to college. I was so nervous about everything related to college, but it had not even occurred to me that my cough would be an issue. Great. And, for the record, I went to an all-girls high school, and I really wanted to date in college. You've gotta love brothers. Do you though?

I have had a horrible cough all my life. It started out as croup and then just kept going. I have moved people from church pews, have had meetings suddenly end, and have been handed thousands of cough drops from the bottom of purses over the years.

Therefore, breathing has always been important to me. Well, I am sure breathing is important to everyone, but when you cannot breathe, you are very aware of creating better breathing environments. So, I have never had the desire to smoke because my lungs are already struggling. I cannot imagine making it worse by smoking. I am also extremely sensitive to environments that may trigger coughing spells. Secondhand smoke feels very first handed when the air around me is a smoke fog.

Every June, I used to celebrate my birthday with my mom and husband in Las Vegas. I love Las Vegas, but I cannot stand smoke, and I do not like it when people around me are drinking lots and swearing.

There is something about Las Vegas being open 24 hours a day that appeals to me though. It feels free.

One such birthday trip, we stopped into a particularly smoky casino. We had been walking in the extremely hot, desert sun, and we needed to rest our feet. What better way to rest than to sit at a blackjack table! While my Mom was at the slot machines and my husband was looking at the sports books, I was at a crowded blackjack table. The other seats had women who looked much older from hard living; they were chain smoking while juggling their cards and their scotches. Now I have lived in Southern California almost all my life, and so I know what smog is. But, on this day on the bar stool at the blackjack table, the smog of smoke was thick, very thick. I had never seen anything like it. I looked around and said to myself, "I have never been this …

How do you think I ended that sentence?

Miserable?

Unhappy?

Unable to breathe?

No, no, and no.

"I have never been this HAPPY!"

Did I just say happy? Am I nuts? Am I happy right now? How could I be happy when I cannot breathe? These women are smoking, swearing, and sour (the three S's). What is making me happy about this situation?

On paper, I had no reason to be happy. But, it turns out that I never felt freer than at that moment. Not one person at that table cared what I was doing. Not one person there was judging me. In fact, I am not sure they even knew I existed. (This time it was okay to not exist in some people's minds.) It was at that moment that I realized my need to feel free was so important that it trumped my need to breathe! I was willing to forego the comfort of clean air for the freedom of not being judged by others. That was quite a lesson for me.

That is a wild hierarchy of needs. Until that moment, I had no idea that I was constantly feeling judged by others, along with judging myself. Can freedom really trump breathing in my world? Who knew!

Comedian Jerry Seinfeld has often shared that the number one fear in life for most people is public speaking. The number two fear on average is death. In a way only Jerry can say, "In other words, at a funeral, you'd rather be the one in the casket than the one giving the eulogy." Public speaking trumps death.

What does your hierarchy of needs look like? What is most important to you? If you had to describe three adjectives that you would like to feel, what would they be? And, in what order would you list them?

OK, let's take this lesson a step further. It turns out that I was not feeling free in my life because of my own judgments. Yes, at the time I was in an environment that was gossipy, judgmental, and petty. But, it was my inability to free myself that was getting to me.

Against the backdrop of those tough women at the blackjack table, even my judgmental self felt better at that table. It was much easier to feel better about myself at that table because I was not drinking scotch, smoking, or swearing. But, I also was not making the best use of my time and money by gambling and staying in a smoky, dark room on a sunny day. So, how many times do we surround ourselves with people who make us feel better only because we compare ourselves to them? Are we with people who are inspiring us to be better, or are we taking it easy because we are with people who are taking the easy road?

You are the average of the five people who surround you. If you want to lose weight, hang out with people who exercise and eat well. If you shop too much, do not go to the mall. Do not tempt yourself. Create your environment that helps you to win.

I learned how to take one of my top adjectives (FREE) and created my environment where that adjective was truest for me. I let go of the gossipy people in my life and surrounded myself with people who made me better. I was able to feel HAPPY against other backdrops where I could also breathe. Who knew how much I could learn from a bad cough! Happy breathing.

Where are you the happiest?

What do you need to change in order to have more of your happy place?

Chapter Fifteen: 24

Our amazing black Labrador was dying the weekend my husband was out of town. While I had been out with my kids, our dog had fallen outside our back porch due to major weakness in her back legs from cancer. Yes, she had fallen and could not get up.

My friend had very recently experienced the death of her black Lab too. Their dog was old and just kind of fell on their bedroom floor. The whole family gathered around as they stroked her. She took her last breath with everyone telling her how much they loved her. As difficult as that was, my friend described it as actually a beautiful experience too. I was convinced that was how our dog would die, in my loving embrace.

Yeah, that is not exactly how it happened. When we got home, I tried to move her into our house. Due to a horrible surgery once, our dog was overly sensitive to her stomach area. She did not want to be moved. So, she was dying on one side of the screen door as I stayed on the floor of our laundry room and spoke to her through the screen door.

This is when our local Blockbuster was down the street. Everyone had been talking about the TV series *24*, and I was late to the game. Right before this infamous weekend, I rented what I thought was Season 1 of the show. "Wow, they don't give you much background and kind of just throw you into the story." I had mistakenly rented Season 4 of the series, and this is one of the most dramatic and violent seasons, which is really saying something.

I knew I had an all-nighter ahead of me because of my dog, and I kept going between my bed with *24* playing and my laundry floor. Looking back now, I remember feeling hazy all night. The distinctive notes of *24*'s theme song played consistently at the beginning of each episode, before and after each commercial, and at the end of every episode. Those notes were either actually playing on the TV or in my mind all night long.

To my surprise, my dog was still alive the next morning. I did not know what to do as she was clearly in so much pain. I had already held the phone up to my dog's ear to have my husband say goodbye, and soon I was going to have two active boys awake and wondering what is happening. I did not know what to do and decided to call the Humane Society. I thought they only came out when animals passed, and they informed me that they could come take our dog. Man, this is so hard to even type this.

I went to the front yard as I saw the truck pull up. My boys were busy with TV and playing, and I had a bit of time to show the man around to the back yard without the boys knowing what was happening. I knew instantly that this was not going to go well after saying hello to the man. I now call him the cop-wanna-be. He did not introduce himself, even though I had introduced myself. He was acting as if this was just another trip to pick up a dead carcass. But, my dog was still alive! This man basically communicated that everything I had done was wrong. I do not remember my friend saying she had to deal with a cop-wanna-be when her dog died in her arms.

Once he had my dog in the truck, hell broke loose. I merely asked what would happen next to my dog. Of course, I was crying, and this man had no idea how to handle a woman's tears. He would not answer the question and then said I owed $60. I had the money in my hand, and as I gave it to him, I said that it was pathetic that I was forced to pay for his torture and horrendous behavior. I asked again what would happen to my dog, and his answer was that if I did not calm down, he was going to call the police. What? I actually said that I thought calling the police might be a good idea. My older son came to the door and saw me crying.

"Mommy, what is happening? Where is our dog? Are they going to take you away? I am scared, Mommy!"

OK, those are the facts, but what you do not know from those facts is the war going on in my mind. I had those stupid *24* notes playing in a continuous loop. I was completely sleep deprived and can still recall the feeling of that fog that seeped into my mind. I just kept staring at the cop-wanna-be's "gun." I think it was probably a stun gun or something, but I could not stop the image of me grabbing his gun and threatening him with it. What would Jack Bauer do at this moment? I just could not stop thinking about it. That video of me taking the gun was so real, in HD, even 3D.

You have to know I am a very, very peaceful person. I have never even touched a real gun. This was so, so out of character for me, but my mind's video was so, so real. Why did I choose this time to binge watch *24*? It took every ounce of energy I had to refrain from this horrific action of grabbing his gun. I was more shocked with these bad thoughts seemingly winning over my own sense of right vs wrong.

I truly feel I was brainwashed. I was poisoned with a deadly cocktail mix of no sleep and violent images. With my sleep deprived mind, I imagined I was in the *24* world; Jack Bauer felt very real to me. It also did not help that the setting of *24* was LA, where I lived!

My son's tears shocked me out of my *24* movie. It was as if I was sleep walking and then suddenly awakened to reality. But, what remains is how powerful brainwashing can be and can sneak up on you. Do you think you are immune to being brainwashed? Do you think this only happens if you are in war zones? Hostages and the military are not the only ones who suffer from being brainwashed.

If you do not think this applies to you, I have two words for you – Old Macdonald. If you had a somewhat normal childhood in the US, most likely there was some part of your brain that automatically said, "Had a farm" when hearing the two words of Old Macdonald. You may have even gone so far to add, "EIEIO." What in the world does EIEIO mean? I looked it up, and aside from some possible computer language with IO, there is no meaning. It does not even make sense to a farmer. It is not even teaching kids the vowels because there are several vowels missing.

It is probably okay that Old Macdonald automatically brings you to a nursery rhyme. (Why is it a rhyme because it does not?) However, what if every day of your childhood you were told you were stupid or ugly? What if everyone told you would not amount to anything? Every. Single, Day. Some people have lived entire childhoods with unfathomable pain. All that I did was binge watch a very farfetched TV series, and I was ready to abandon everything that I knew was right.

It would take a lot of repetition to break the Old Macdonald automatic thought from your mind, and that is just a nursery rhyme. That is why it takes a lot of positive repetition to break the long-established patterns to old habits. Your environment has to be all encompassing to bolster your new thoughts that work for you.

Taking an active role in changing the past takes work, but it absolutely can be done.

Alcoholics determined to stop drinking eventually realizes that changes to their environment are key to success. They probably need to find a new group of friends. Most of their old social circle are likely spending a lot of time drinking. Plus, when someone gets sober, it changes the dynamic of the group. It might force some to take a look at their drinking, and let's just say usually there is some reluctance.

In my social work training, I really could not grasp the idea that some people, especially in the same family, might not celebrate an alcoholic's path to sobriety. Everyone serves a role in the extended family. I work with clients who are oblivious to the roles they still play in their extended family. Even though they are adults with families of their own, the roles in the extended family rarely change. The attention that was demanded by the alcoholic kept others from looking at their own problems. Once an alcoholic becomes sober, that excuse is no longer there, forcing people to look within. Family members sometimes sabotage a person's efforts to improve themselves because of the possible consequences.

This is not just true of alcoholics. In order for anyone to change, they have to be able to let go of unhealthy habits. They have to change their environment and find new circles. Their focus is in making positive changes. Old patterns need to be broken. It is important to recognize your need to be strong because there can be resistance, especially from loved ones.

This is usually how the cycle goes:

1. Feeling responsible for fixing others' problems,

2. Tired at the weight of responsibility,

3. Anger at extended family members (usually parents) for not getting what was needed as a child,

4. Letting go of expectations for family members to give you what they are not capable of giving, and

5. Defining what is missing and finding ways to get the missing pieces for yourself.

What is your role you play in your family dynamics?

What do you want to change?

What is holding you back from changing?

Chapter Sixteen: True to Self

At the fourth-grade parent & teacher meeting for my son, I started in with my usual speech I gave all of his teachers. I explained how my son is internally harder on himself than they could ever be on him. Basically, I was asking for them to go easy on him because they had to know his internal pressure cooker was on high.

"Do you?" That was this teacher's response to my speech.

"Do I what?"

"Do you ever veer outside the box?"

I just stared at him. We were not talking about me; we were talking about how hard my child is on himself. Maybe if your son saw you living outside of that wound-up box, he would go easier on himself. That was not in quotes because that was not technically what the teacher said, but it was the message of what he meant.

All I could do was stare at him. No one had ever said that to me, but this teacher was exactly right. He had given me a gift I will never forget. That happened over ten years ago, but I can vividly picture myself sitting on that small chair in his classroom. So, what did I do next? I enrolled both my sons and me in a drawing class. I must say I hated every minute of drawing but loved every minute with my boys. It taught me how to enjoy life outside of the box of self-criticism and how to go easy on myself.

My rule of role modeling what I wanted to teach my boys was not being lived out, and this teacher saw that pressure immediately. I was exemplifying to my boys that it was okay to be wound up so tightly.

How could I teach my boys grace and self-forgiveness when I rarely gave those qualities to myself?

The acorn really does not fall far from the tree. Children learn so many subtle messages by how parents care for themselves and others. Children are watching family's every move to make sure what they say matches what they do.

It has taken me a lot, Lot, LOT of years to learn the lesson, but true freedom and really taking care of yourself are not always fun. You do not always have to enjoy the nourishment your body needs to function well. You cannot just eat what makes you feel good at that moment, but sacrificing now for better future feelings is the best kind of freedom. I rebelled against feeling controlled by doing what I thought felt good at that moment. A Diet Coke in my hand at all times instead of boring water, a bear claw for breakfast, and an all carb dinner do not make me feel any freer.

There is a real cost to not honoring your promises to yourself. Broken promise after broken promise is a slow death to trusting yourself. Just like when a child lies to a parent, the parent admonishes that the trust has to be earned back. Disloyalty to one's self is equally damaging. Daily honoring self-promises restores the trust. When you see sacrifices as more about honoring yourself, the hardship of the sacrifice dissipates.

"Well... I think that...It's that if I ever go looking for my heart's desire again, I won't look any farther than my own back yard because if it isn't there, I never really lost it to begin with."
— Dorothy in the Wizard of Oz by L. Frank Baum

Part III: The Top Ten List

In Part I, the top ten ingredients of anxiety were introduced. This part is to fully understand these individual ingredients against your problem. The reality is that we all suffer from all of these ingredients to some extent periodically throughout life. It is just that those who suffer from anxiety tend to have more of these ingredients happening at the same time and in greater magnitude.

Take a look at your top problem and how each of these ingredients is contributing to your problem. By recognizing the ingredients, you can reshape the ingredients to solve your problem.

Chapter Seventeen: Perfectionism

Perfectionism is a thief. Perfectionism, which is unattainable, is the thief of getting better. One cannot recognize improvements under the umbrella of perfectionism because small steps forward still do not result in the perfect destination. The finish line is constantly moving.

The dangling carrot of perfection cannot be reached, making it difficult to feel loved. Most anxiety sufferers see their self-worth through what they do for others... perfectly. It is quite the burden to carry. Loving yourself is strictly dependent on how well you perform for others. Usually those with anxiety equate their actions to the right to earn others' love. Ironically, it is not until we embrace our own flaws and allow ourselves the grace and space to fail that we can feel loved.

From where does this need for perfection come? Typically, one has had a past, usually childhood, where they equated being worthy of love with how well they followed the rules, how well they did in school, and/or what they did for someone else. A strict parent can want the best for a child, but that child can easily misread a parent's actions. Strictness can be mistaken for equating love with a perfectly done task. Love becomes conditional on what you do for others. It is a pattern of seeing behavior as definition that you love someone and that someone loves you in return.

I do not like it when one questions if another is a perfectionist. Even if they are not a perfectionist, what person is going to admit that they are not? Striving for perfection is right up there with multitasking. They are mistaken as badges of honor. Everyone thinks the answer to efficiency is multitasking. However, it is when you are singly focused on one task for a block of time that you take on the task with greater depth and efficiency. If we see perfectionism as a badge of honor, we are left feeling that nothing is ever fully accomplished. We cannot let go, and "good enough" is nonexistent.

Perfectionism and procrastination are ugly stepsisters. We usually put off what we do not want to do, and we usually do not want to do what we do not know HOW to do. Looking foolish is the last way we want to appear, especially to ourselves. Those who suffer from low self-esteem particularly are not interested in engaging in another activity to prove they are not capable in yet one more way. But, if we have the freedom to do things just for the enjoyment of them no matter how they turn out, we are more likely to kick the procrastination fears to the curb. We will get more done if we know that failure is likely and not a crisis. The truest of learning comes from failure.

With each new effort, find your takeaway. I have many clients who demand perfection from themselves. For whatever new skill they are trying to master, I make sure to remind them that the real learning usually comes from getting it wrong.

1. The first thing that they have to do to master a new skill is to actually do it. Action is a must.

2. The next step is analyzing the results from the attempt. What felt right? What felt weird? What is not sitting right from within you?

3. WHAT IS YOUR GUT TELLING YOU? It is only until you are ready to listen to your instincts that the real magic lessons get learned. Soon you will have ample practice at your particular skill, where you will make improvements with each practice.

4. What are you going to do differently next time?

Repeated action through tweaking is the best prescription to overcoming the need to get it right the first time. If you continue to demand getting it perfect the first time, you will continue to rob yourself of improvements over time. By practicing, you will automatically be showing yourself grace because you will see each practice session as building muscles. You will just keep getting better. Do not let perfectionism rob you of the joy of better.

Chapter Eighteen: People Pleaser

When do you know people have fully pleased? Is your job of pleasing people ever done? There just does not seem to be an end to the process. Have you convicted yourself to a life sentence to please others?

You do not have to be found guilty of a never-ending cycle of pleasing people. You can break the pattern when you learn that you have almost zero control on how others feel about you. Plus, if they love the person you are pretending to be, what happens when you let your guard down?

People pleasing is actually quite a selfish activity. What? Yes, people pleasing is actually not an accurate description of what is happening. We are spending lots of energy trying to control everyone's opinion of us. It is the ultimate control freak move. It should instead be called I Pleasers because we are trying to control how others see us, which in turn will come back to how we see ourselves. People pleasers, where I should have been the President, CEO, and Board Chairman, are pretending to be only a different personality in order to belong to a group of people or be tied to a person. In order to be seen as cool, I have to pretend to be someone I am not in order to win the affections of people who ironically also are not who they seem to be. But, it is selfish because when we pretend to highlight one aspect of ourselves as the full definition of us, it is what WE want ourselves to be. If I can fool them into thinking I am cool, I will feel cool myself.

People pleasers (PPs) are very convinced they will not be loved for who they truly are. So, they feel compelled to wear a costume. The reason it is a selfish move is that people pleasers try to be a certain way in hopes their image will come back like a boomerang.

We are all multi-faceted, but we also have a default image of ourselves as who we truly are. Tony Robbins calls it our Emotional Home. We are so afraid of the real us to come out that we create a false sense of identity. The process of living is to make that false identity so real that we fool everyone, including ourselves. Whenever we feel our default personality has been discovered, it is like the shame Adam and Eve felt when they found out they were naked. Adam and Eve were happy being their truest selves because they did not know they "should" be anything other than themselves. It was only until they disobeyed that they felt shame at being naked.

Think of the power of Oz before the curtain was drawn. He was the all-powerful Oz. Deep down he knew who he was, but his costume and mask were so powerful that even he believed his fantasy. If Oz could no longer be seen by others as the all-powerful Oz, he could not continue to live the dream.

So, how should PPs change the process? Instead of changing how we think others see us (which we now know is not in our control), we should make sure we absolutely love our healthy Emotional Home. All of our energy should be put into being always comfortable with ourselves. Usually people's Emotional Homes are not positive defaults but are homes built out of our deep insecurities. I know someone who has an Emotional Home of worry. My father's Emotional Home was that he was not smart. My Emotional Home USED TO BE (that is one big high five to myself) that I was bad to my core. The costume I put on was needing to be perfect to be loved. Yes, I moved my Emotional Home. It took a lot of work, but I did it. You can too.

Where is your Emotional Home? What first came to your mind when you read that question? If you are not sure, when you experience a loss or pain, what are your default thoughts? Where do you feel insecure? What do you protectively hold, fearing you will be found a fraud?

How is your Emotional Home working for you? (I hope you read that with a Dr. Phil voice in your head.) You really can change it. People pleasing is the procrastination of confronting and changing your Emotional Home. Take off the costume. If your default or your mind's home is not working for you, MOVE.

Chapter Nineteen: Procrastination

Would you like to know how much mental energy you exhaust by blaming yourself for what you have not been doing? How much of our self-talk is spent judging how we are spending our time? I call this process Stealing Time. Instead of doing what we think we should be doing, we do what we want but just feel guilty while doing it. When we are unable to fully enjoy our "down time," we are holding that time hostage. Stealing Time could also be called Robbing Joy.

Likely, your pattern of procrastination has existed for an awfully long time. Where you procrastinate has changed over time, but there is likely a long history of avoiding pain. You may be so used to this nagging thief of joy in some part of your brain that you hardly recognize it. Have you ever had a time in your life when you were not avoiding SOMETHING? I have actually said to myself in the past, "Wait. Hold on. I am worried because I forgot what was worrying me." Since I rarely had a peaceful moment without worrying about something, it felt like something was majorly wrong when I was completely at peace. As you are reading this now, I am here to tell you the time has come where you can learn how to live without some constant, mental energy of worry.

If you put the stealing on hold for a minute and show yourself grace by looking at WHERE you are procrastinating, you can turn procrastination into a window of opportunity to learn about your fears. Once you are aware of what really frightens you, then you can address those fears. Of course, it all comes down to figuring out what that negative self-talk reinforces. Imposter syndrome, fears of inadequacy, fears of not deserving success, etc. are all general fears that keep you playing small. It is much more difficult to attack a moving target. When we lump our fears into generality, we cannot address specific fears. For example, if you have convinced yourself you are not enough in all areas, there is truly little incentive to make small progress. I choose "not enough" as an example because almost everyone feels inadequate in some area. If we think our entire being is inadequate or if we cannot let go of a childhood label, we cannot seem to progress in any area.

Since you just learned about the family connection between procrastination and perfectionism (ugly stepsisters), you know now the pull of putting off certain tasks because of the confirmation that you are not measuring up. If you believe you cannot feel self-worth until you do all tasks perfectly, there is zero incentive to do work at all. However, if you recognize that there is no pressure to get it right the first time, the pressure valve on that one time is off.

I love to assign homework in my counseling work, and the more creative the assignment, the more likely my clients will complete the tasks. For my clients who love to study, worksheets might be their thing. For my clients who love sports, if I can figure out a way to turn my fun homework into a game, then I am almost ensuring success at trying homework. It depends on how my clients see homework and what motivates them. I personally respond well to games that do not have a winner and loser but games that encourage me to make "better" steps forward in self-improvement.

All of my homework though is geared to being exceptionally kind to oneself. I have not assigned it yet, but I would love to assign that a client needs to craft each day but also to make as many mistakes as possible in their crafts. There really is something to be said for doing a task just for the joy of the task regardless of the outcome. As I continue to explain here that you learn much more from your mistakes, you have to relieve that pressure valve of perfectionism. If we just have to hand in proof that we have spent quality time crafting but with zero judgment on how we have crafted, we can turn our time into truly free time. Our mental energy is free from the constant reminder to be somewhere else.

There is an endless supply of advice on how to beat procrastination and tackling your "should" list, but as with any advice, you have to make the solution your own. Find what works best for you, but my only directive is to have FUN with your list. One time a friend asked me on why I could not just do a mundane task but had to put my kind of spin on it. He thought I made everything more difficult than it needed to be. While I think it was a criticism posing as a question, I turned the question into a compliment. He was absolutely right. While there are only a few ways of doing the laundry, I had to find a fun way to encourage me to do the laundry. Instead of continuing to berate myself for not getting a task done, I ask myself how I can make it my own. Anyone can do the dishes or the laundry, but can you have fun doing it?

Anything that gets us thinking positively of our future is a great exercise. We should spend some daily time making tomorrow easier. This is especially true for finances, but that is a separate topic for another book. It is possible to enjoy time without a part of your brain nagging you to spend time elsewhere. Check in with yourself on how you are feeling when you are spending down time. If you are feeling guilty for making that time your own and not working, get up and satisfy that urge to spend a small block of time on work. There are times when I limit how much WORK I am allowed to do for a project or for the day. Once I have hit that time limit, I am not allowed to work anymore that day. This gives me huge incentive to make the most of the time I am dedicating to work. Most people limit how much free time they get or that they cannot spend that time until work is done. However, I just did the opposite. In other words, I made even the concept of how I procrastinate my own.

Chapter Twenty: Pain of the Past

I once had a client in their eighties seek therapy. He was struggling with how he was treated compared to his sibling when they were children. It was not any kind of abusive situation, but he felt less than or not enough. Each time I opened the door to the past, he quickly closed the door and passed off his look back as just research. After several failed attempts to examine what was really bothering him, he stopped seeking help. He said he had enough research and thanked me for my time. His pain, though some seventy years ago, felt very alive and real, almost as if it had happened yesterday. I am sure it did feel like yesterday or today for him all the time in his own mind because he continued to carry it around with him. But, he was not ready to examine it. Even at eighty years old, it was too tough to face the fear.

The process does have to happen when you are ready. How do you know if you are ready? To quote Dave Ramsey, "When you are sick and tired of being sick and tired, you will make the change." When the secondary gains of keeping the pain (and there are always gains in keeping the pain) are no longer as important as the gains of giving up the past pain, you are probably ready.

Almost every time I ask clients what benefit there is in keeping their pain, the first response is that there is no benefit. If that were true though, your brain would have realized it was time to move to a more secure location awhile ago. It might not be clear at first, and the gain is probably not even in your conscious mind. Not examining the real problems from the past may be protecting you from the unknown. Never discount the power from fear of the unknown. The brain hates to not be in control, and the brain feels it is better to confront a known enemy than an unknown one.

There can be a number of reasons why you might not want to let go of past pain. You probably need to process it with someone to figure out what gains there are in keeping the past. But, when you are ready, you will see that there is a real freedom when you start tearing down the past's prison walls. You will be able to use your past as your best teacher instead of living as a prisoner. Use your past.

When you feel convicted of something (convicted = conflicted on steroids) and just cannot let something go, there is a lesson to be learned still. Stay with the pain because your secret path to joy will soon be revealed. On a trip to Maui, we once took the long winding Road to Hana. It did not have to be that long of a winding road, but my husband insisted that we buy a CD that mapped out the many side paths along the journey. We had seen many waterfalls and experienced jungle terrain with lots of foreign noises.

The final destination was seen in light of what we had experienced along the way. We took so many side excursions that once we got to the final destination, we were so relieved to have made it. For others, the trip was not that long but also not as rich as it was for us. That is how I liken the process of learning our lessons. We have to take many diversions to get to the final destination, but we are at a higher plateau because of the journey. We also have made a lot of judgments about the world based on our previous experiences. Some of those judgments are no longer serving or protecting us, and they have to be examined and changed.

The Bible (Proverbs 22:7) teaches, "The rich rule over the poor, and the borrower is slave to the lender." An unexamined past owns you. Just like debt, you can be a slave to the past. Lose the chains that bind you to a past that has not been reconciled. If something from your past caused you to view the world or yourself in a certain way and that way is no longer working for you, you do not have to serve a life sentence. Set yourself free.

The harder we try to control how others see us, the more we are shown it is out of our hands. In fact, it is none of our business how others see us. They are looking at us through their own lenses filled with their insecurities. That is why it is so powerful to learn someone else's story of pain from their past. How they see life currently is fully shaped by their past. By walking in someone else's shoes for just a moment, we learn to take very little personally. We can be here for each other to help one another grow and learn from the past. Our pain can be transformed into beautiful tools for serving our futures and purpose.

Chapter Twenty-One: Heightened Sense of Responsibility

The title alone of this book indicates how dysfunctional a sense of responsibility can become if left unattended. Service to other people's problems is one of the greatest pains of feeling hyper-responsible. Most responsible people think of their sense of responsibility as a curse instead of a blessing because of years of feeling unappreciated and used. When others know you will be responsible, they are "off the hook." They can sit back and relax because it is your shift. Responsible people rarely can turn it off; the mind is always working. When one's sense of responsibility is left unchecked, boundaries become very squishy or nonexistent.

When people abuse others' sense of responsibility, they are relinquishing control for themselves. From the point of view of the responsible person, taking over the issues, problems, and situations that belong to others means that the cycle of enabling continues. Responsible people in others' business rob others of the opportunity to learn their own lessons.

We have to solve our own problems. Responsible people have to learn to stay in their own lane. My heightened sense of responsibility has been a constant thorn. Even though I love Gallup's Strengths Awareness, I was sooooo disappointed in RESPONSIBLE being my #1 strength. I worked diligently to lessen its impact and to focus on my other top four strengths. Responsible people carry a cross and simply need to be reminded that they can let down others' crosses. They MUST let go of others' crosses in order to feel peace in being in charge of themselves alone.

One of life's dangers that is rarely recognized is what happens to responsible people when they are placed amongst others who accept ZERO responsibility for emotional issues. When people do not hold up their roles in a social group, it is very common for sensitive, vigilant others to accept full responsibility. This is especially true in family dynamics. When one person refuses to accept responsibility for their own pain they are causing, there are usually others who are unfortunately, subconsciously accepting the blame. For example, individuals who have personality disorders usually make others' lives very difficult. All life and all oxygen can be absorbed from the room. Think of anyone with narcissistic tendencies. There is a lot of drama and a lot of focus on them. Responsible people usually pick up the slack. It is so important to recognize the dynamics happening with dramatic relationships. If you suffer from anxiety and have a heightened sense of responsibility, look at your relationships to see if you are absorbing others' needs, neglecting your own needs, and blurring the boundaries.

The hardest part of letting go of responsibility is the sense of purpose and meaning these roles play in the responsible person's world. Anyone who is hyper-responsible for others' problems takes pride and derives meaning from their calling. That makes it much harder to justify giving up responsibility for others' issues. "I am the only one who can do it right," is the underlying attitude. It is difficult giving up control for others' problems because that then forces the responsible person to look at their own issues. Where is the fun in that?

Chapter Twenty-Two: Lack of Boundaries

"Boundaries are an ultimate life hack. They'll give you space to protect your energy. You'll feel less overwhelm and daily stress. Confidence and self-esteem will start to build. Relationships will hold more meaning... Boundaries are your firm line... Almost everyone struggles with boundaries because they never saw the adults in their family have them."
— Dr. Nicole LePera, the Holistic Psychologist

If you really want to learn about boundaries, I highly suggest taking a journey with Dr. Henry Cloud in his book called *Boundaries*. I think of Dr. Cloud as the boundaries guru. Dr. Cloud encourages us to think of boundaries as property lines. We have access to allowing others in as we wish. A lack of boundaries is one of my top ten ingredients for anxiety because of how much those who suffer from anxiety look outside of themselves for answers. With the other ingredients of people pleasing and a heightened sense of responsibility, there is huge emphasis on looking to others for meaning and a sense of purpose.

When we don't know where our lane ends, we don't know what is ours vs. theirs. Then, when we finally decide to take care of ourselves, we usually feel so guilty or so undeserving of our own space. When we continue to put on others' oxygen masks instead of our own, we die. Getting a handle on one's boundaries brings permission to put on the oxygen mask first.

A lack of boundaries usually has everything to do with equating our self-worth and self-value by what we DO for others. Most of my clients tell me that they want their significant other to feel a certain way about them, and they focus on what they do for others to give them almost a guarantee that their significant other will stay in the relationship. "After all I did for him, he has the nerve to leave?" "I put my whole life on hold to raise these kids, and this is how they thank me?"

Continually sacrificing our self-value to our actions for others inevitably brings bitterness and resentment to the relationship. How many times do we fall into the trap ourselves of blaming others for our own decisions to sacrifice our priorities? As much as we try to not let resentment creep into our relationships, it is inevitable when we continue to limit our value to our actions. The resentment plays out against others, but it is actually anger from within for not staying true to ourselves.

Recently I have been working with clients who feel backed into a corner in their relationships. They are being manipulated and pressured, and the manipulators are people who have been in my clients' lives a long time. This further increases the confusion my clients have because my clients have gone along with the manipulation for years.

The time has come to stop defining your value by what you do for others. Ironically, when you come to accept that emotional boundaries are healthy and necessary, what you do for others improves. Serving others no longer becomes at the expense of your goals, your desires, and your self-worth. You won't feel used because you will give out of the sheer joy of giving to others, not from obligation to improve your self-worth.

Honoring your emotional boundaries is a process of earning back trusting yourself. In the words of Martha Stewart, "that is a very good thing." Every time you look to others for self-worth, you evade trusting yourself. By focusing on your unique strengths, goals, purpose, and mission, you naturally give of yourself. Your property line is well-defined and beautiful. It is acceptance of yourself and staying true to your uniqueness.

Chapter Twenty-Three: Extreme Expectations

"Hard on self" is how almost every one of my clients describes themselves to me. Like multitasking and perfectionism, extreme expectations have to be reshaped NOT as a badge of honor. Even though being hard on oneself can also be a motivator to get a lot done, easing off the pressure pedal creates peace of mind.

Originally, I was going to label this ingredient as Extreme Expectations of Self. However, I have found that usually anxiety sufferers have high expectations for others too, but usually not at the extreme level. When people with high self-expectations encounter others who are not tightly wound, envy is inevitable. How come they get to be off the hook to not expect as much of themselves?

Before I was able to recognize how hard I was on myself, I would find myself very envious of others who were able to not focus on others' expectations. It seemed like I was consumed with fulfilling what I THOUGHT others expected me to do. The reality was that these expectations were only in my mind. I rarely checked in with others to see if they were holding me to high standards. It is really such an unfair practice. I would hold others responsible for them expecting me to over-deliver, but these were usually expectations that only existed in my mind.

We hold off on feeling we deserve love until we meet these extreme expectations, and this process usually develops early in life. We are just continuing the pattern unless we learn to recognize how hard it makes our lives. Our minds place us at the center of the universe when we are young. As we are trying to make sense of the universe and our place in it, we assume we are the pilot in control. It is too scary to leave life up to fate or in someone else's control, and so we learn to expect a lot from ourselves. For example, while it is very painful for a young child to think they caused their parents' fights or divorce, it does put the child in control. A known fear beats fear of the unknown almost every time. If we think our actions alone can deliver us from pain, we learn to exceed expectations.

This sense of control unfortunately feeds the expectations. There is a whole play with a large cast of characters playing in one's mind when we imagine others' expectations for us. We end up holding the actual people accountable for these made-up expectations in our minds. Again, resentment and envy creep into relationships because we are consumed with the weight of what we have created ourselves.

It is very difficult to let go of extreme expectations because it feels like then you will not be productive or not have incentive to stretch and challenge yourself. This pressure though is further evidence that you are equating your self-worth to what you do, how well you perform, and how much you give to others. Your self-worth is in who you are, not what you do or expect yourself to do.

People of faith are much better able to understand the connection to their self-worth and who they are instead of what they do. When you believe you are a child of God's, you know He loves you unconditionally. Plus, through the act of forgiveness, you know God forgives you for your sins. Now if only you could master self-forgiveness!

Releasing yourself from expectations is yet one more way to be exceptionally kind to yourself. Let's make sure you are releasing yourself from the right area though. You are no longer trying to meet a model or a higher version of a generic person. You are releasing yourself from being that perfect person so that you can be YOUR OWN person. You are holding yourself to the extreme expectations to be yourself. You will love all parts of you in order to celebrate your uniqueness.

Chapter Twenty-Four: Martha Stewart of Crafting Slightest Hint of Criticism

The anxiety sufferer can be as creative as Martha Stewart when it comes to crafting someone else's words into criticism. The hottest button is pushed when an anxiety sufferer thinks they are being criticized, and unfortunately, a lot of words feel critical. Society has no idea how critical an anxiety sufferer's mind is already. Their minds believe that they need to protect themselves by judging themselves with terribly negative self-talk. Yes, that does not make too much sense on paper, but it is a long-established pattern of negative judgments. Any hint by an outsider of criticism sends the mind into panic. It feels like their worst-case scenario is coming true.

Just knowing that you can overreact to others' words should provide some relief. Knowing that you can hear their words differently without that self-defensive tone is freeing in itself. As much as I am encouraging you to silence the self-critical voice, I'm also encouraging you to give others credit for good intentions. Their words are more likely encouragement and support and not given with mal intent. On paper, we know that the mind is constantly looking for danger zones. You can hear one hundred praises, but it is that one, vague statement that feels it could be criticism. The mind thinks about it and soon crafts it into a huge, personal weakness.

Dr. David Burns wonderfully organizes our craftiness into ten cognitive distortions. The overall process though is that the mind is desperately trying to protect oneself by finding all danger zones. When we understand that what everyone says is more about them than it is us, we can release our own pressure valve.

Just because someone gives us a label or criticizes us does not mean that we have to accept the reality of what has been said or given. With an emotional shield up first, we are able to evaluate if their words have personal meaning or validity for us. If we decide that their words have merit for us, we have learned a lesson that we can apply to the future. Plus, we can apologize for our part. However, if we have decided that their label or critique is not valid for us, we are not mandated to accept it.

Of course, this is much easier than said. It is especially difficult to not absorb a parent's label or criticism as a character flaw. Protecting yourself temporarily in the past may have meant that you accepted criticism, but that pattern of AUTOMATICALLY accepting any criticism can stop. As I mentioned in the chapter on labels, my dream is that every adult gives themselves permission to let go of old or incorrect labels. You may feel particularly triggered to accept certain criticisms over others automatically, but only you know what critiques build you up to doing better instead of merely tearing you down. You can learn to know the difference once you create an emotional barrier. You can evaluate then if it is in your best, future interests to learn from a critique or to deflect it as invalid to you.

If you do not feel worthy of accepting the praises, you cannot then be allowed to accept the blame. Remember mistakes are our invitations to improve. You are just finding more ways to get to your truest and most unique self!

Chapter Twenty-Five: Negative Self-Talk

I used to have the meanest BFF. She was always putting me down, was always telling me where I went wrong, and was never giving me any credit. I really did not think I deserved a better friend. After all, by pointing out all of my flaws, I was keeping my enemies closer. Yes, this BFF was the "friend" in my own mind. There was an angel on one shoulder with a devil on the other, but it was my mind that worried me the most. My internal GPS was doing a fine job of getting me to my destinations of accomplishments, but oh, the toll it was taking to get there.

I once had a client where we were doing some budgeting and financial coaching. She told me what she estimated what she was spending each month, and I told her that based on what we had previously discussed, I thought it was much more than what she thought. In fact, I told her I thought it was probably more like double or triple what she thought. Without any kind of tracking of her spending, she only assumed her mind's calculations were correct. After all, she had money in the bank, right? Another client told me that I did not need to reconcile her bank activity each month with her business because she knew what she was making all right here, as she pointed to her forehead. Yeah, okay, right. It turned out that the woman with the budget was spending three times more than what she calculated overall, and we never really did find out about my business client's books because they were such a mess.

If you are not actually tracking your spending, you do not really know the numbers. Why am I talking about financial items here? It is because you do not really know how negative your mind's self-talk is until you start really listening and tracking it. We cannot change what we do not know exists. When our thought patterns have been created and have evolved since childhood, we are not even aware of what thought patterns exist. These thought patterns get filed away into our subconscious and become very automatic without recognition. It is not until we start listening that we realize how negative and pervasive the self-talk is. Our real friends would never treat us this way, or we would have left the relationship a long time ago. Plus, your mind is with you ALL THE TIME. Your mind is like the last friend at the party who just will not take a hint to go home. They never leave. Like spending money, I think the negative self-talk is a lot worse than you realize.

This chapter on negative self-talk is so negative! However, please know this is all fixable. What is the best way? Really? You do not know the answer by now, after getting this far in the book ? I have clients actually tell me, "I know. I know. I had this Edie voice in my head following me around reminding me to show myself grace and self-forgiveness." Yes, the best defense against a mean BFF is to shower them with kindness.

You will learn more steps later in the book, but for now, turn Negative Nate/Nancy into Nice Nate/Nancy by saying at least five positive thoughts for every unkind thought. Seriously, five! It will be a hassle to stop what you are doing and think of five positive thoughts, and maybe (hopefully) that exercise alone will train you to stop the negativity. Be the best kind of BFF, the one that laughs with you and helps you.

I have this very weird quirk that I have laughing fits. What I consider funny will soon turn into your worst nightmare if you are with me because I. CAN'T. STOP. LAUGHING. Seriously, priests have stopped Masses, and friends have threatened to leave me without a drive home. I know what I find funny, but sometimes even I didn't understand why I was laughing so uncontrollably. I did not understand why something not quite THAT funny would start a twenty-minute laughing/crying spree. Once I started to look at when I was having laughing fits, I realized many fits happened right after a heightened period of stress. I did not even realize I was going through as much stress as I was until I had the laughing fit. It was like my "tell," but it was after the fact.

My laughing fits now have transformed into windows of opportunity to review my past stress but also how my negative self-talk might have contributed to the stress. What have I been saying to myself about the stressful time, and could I have improved the time by being kinder to myself? Do not get me wrong. Even if I kick negative self-talk to the curb, I will still have laughing fits. I will just enjoy them more!

Listen to the self-talk. Be exceptionally kind to yourself. Be a true BFF. When in doubt, laugh.

Chapter Twenty-Six: Control

To gain any understanding of anxiety, control has to be analyzed. Every person I have met who suffers from anxiety, including myself, struggles to understand what comprises their sense of control. Most anxiety sufferers describe themselves as "control freaks." I think that label alone shows the confusion around one's area of influence. All of the rules anxiety sufferers create are ways to gain control over their environment. And, like a sense of responsibility, they can let their own senses spill into others' territories. Our heightened sense of responsibility can force us to feel responsible for others' problems. Our sense of control for ourselves spills over into trying to control our environments and others' actions.

This book is titled Serving Others' Penance because the best of intentions on feeling responsible can run amok. That is the same with a heightened sense of control. In trying to make one's world orderly, organized, and in control. it is easy for the boundaries into others' worlds to be crossed or obliterated in some cases. For example, someone with severe Obsessive Compulsive Disorder (OCD) may have a rule that all dishes have to be washed thoroughly a very specific way. When someone in the family does not conform to the severe rules of washing. what is the right answer? Throwing out the rules upsets the one with OCD; conforming to obsessive rules that do not make sense to the family members invades everyone else's freedom. Just ignoring the rules creates panic and a complete loss of control for the person with OCD. The release of control has to be done with care and compassion. Ironically, restoring the rules of behavior to just the creator of the rules makes the anxious sufferer much less dependent on the obsessions. However, the process has to be done gingerly and usually with the help of a therapist skilled in understanding the rules behind OCD. This is not a book about

OCD specifically, but I think it is easier to understand how a sense of control can get out of hand when considering the rules behind OCD.

The standard objection to meditation is that most find it too hard to stay focused on... well, nothing. Usually, we are so hard on ourselves to get mediation done perfectly the first few times that we soon give up. Once someone explained the meditation process in a way that showed me grace, I was able to meditate. They gave me the gift of thinking of meditation as being a spectator of a parade. During meditation, the parade is of our thoughts. We watch as our thoughts smoothly pass along the parade route. Uh-oh, once we start focusing on one thought, the parade stops. We have backed up the parade by focusing on one part in particular. To get the parade flowing again, we start to just observe our different thoughts passing along our minds.

This is exactly what happens when our energy gets blocked in our system. We have stopped the parade by focusing on one area. When we fear we cannot control a certain area, we begin trying to gain control in other areas. If we feel ill equipped in one area, we are hyper-focused into other territories to gain control. People-pleasing mode is usually an indication of a dysfunctional sense of control and a lack of self-esteem. "If I control how others see me, I will get that reflected back onto me and feel good about myself." That thought is usually in the mind of the person who lacks an internal sense of controlling one's feelings. When they realize that they have ZERO control on how others see them, they tend to stop looking to others to give themselves what they most need. You can begin to rely on yourself.

Ironically, it is not until one admits they are not in control of how others see them that they gain their own personal sense of control over themselves. Their self-esteem is no longer dependent on anyone else but themselves. After all, we usually cling to controlling others when we feel out of control over ourselves. When we focus more on how we need no one else to feel good, the pressure to control dissipates. Dependence within relationships and control are cousins. When we alone feel we NEED another for any reason, we have lost some of our own control. However, the flip side is heavenly. When we learn that our relationships are pure love without dependence, then the need to control outside of oneself is usually unnecessary. Loving without needing removes the need to control.

Part IV: The M.A.P. Map Anxiety's Past

Present anxiety has majorly strong roots in the past. Traveling back in time reshapes the emotional reaction to the past. I travel by Four Winds, which not coincidentally is the name of the make of my RV. The four winds represent the four steps that I created as a blueprint to turn your stories into tools for your best future, your better self.

Learn how to stop serving others' penance, and instead learn to see your stories as power. Yes, even the stories (actually, ESPECIALLY the stories) of pain from your past can be positively powerful!

Your four steps with eight verbs are:

1. Learn. Define.
2. Trust. Tell.
3. Value. Let go.
4. Write. Change.

To give more meat to these steps, they specifically are:

1. Learn everything about yourself. This is the time to invest in learning who YOU think you are and not the labels that have been given to you. Define your top adjectives, your top values, and your top red flags.

2. Trust in your instincts and your gut. Tell the truth by living the truth everywhere, especially within.

3. Value yourself in who you are and not only by what you do. Then, let go. Set yourself free by letting go of self-imposed limitations and others' opinions and expectations.

4. Write the story of your past. Then, write the story of your future self as if you are writing your own obituary. Make the obituary one fabulous story. Once you have your two stories – one of the past and one of the future, change your environment and thinking in order to get closer each day to that fabulous, future person.

Four steps, that on paper sound much easier to do, will be the foundation for creating your best life. You will be showing yourself grace through the journey, and you will no longer be detained by your past. You will be traveling the road to peace of mind knowing that you are fulfilling God's plan, specifically designed for you.

Does everyone have to do this examination of their past? Not necessarily, but a general rule of thumb to follow is whether or not you are able to solve your current problems. If you have tried, and I mean really tried, to improve your current situation but there are forces still holding you back, you probably are limited with the meaning you've given to life based on your past experiences. If you find yourself wondering if you are sabotaging yourself, you likely need to examine what about your past is holding you back from happiness.

Chapter Twenty-Seven: Learn, and Define

"I was sitting next to my four year-old son on the couch watching TV. He turned to me and said, 'Dad, when I grow up, I want to be a doctor.' Yes, yes, yes. I am doing so well in this parenting thing. My son is going to be a doctor. A few minutes later he turned to me and said, 'Or a dinosaur.'"
— Michael Jr.

LEARN

Even though I am trying not to encourage you to become obsessive, this is my one exception. Become obsessive in learning about you.

What makes you tick? What do you like? What do you not like, and why do you think you learned to not like it? This is so much more than a job interview about your strengths and weaknesses; it has to do with what motivates you. Are you having trouble describing yourself? Like the Sound of Music, let's start at the very beginning. I will not get all Freudian on you here, but your childhood is the key to unlocking how you have been shaped. This shape can be remolded of course, or there would not be much point in having this book. You absolutely can break the bonds that bind you. First though, you must know what those bonds are. What did you love to do as a child? What was your default – TV, books, outside time? What did you want to be when you grew up? If you can look at what you wanted to be at around the age of eight, that was the beginning. They say there is lots of clarity around the age of eight as you are coming into your own person. Is your current profession close to that early desire, or what do you think brought you off that track? What did you love to do as a child? Do you still love sports or hobbies or music? Do you still have passions and feel a purpose for a greater good?

When I was young, I wanted to not be confined to one profession. The idea that I would have my eggs all in one basket in terms of a profession was very stifling and limiting for me. I wanted to try a bit of a lot of professions. How did things work out? Well, I have taught cotillion, tennis, math, and accounting. I have worked at a fabric store and now have my own craft store. I have been an auditor, a tax preparer, a social worker, a therapist, and a coach. I am a university professor and now an author. That closed-in feeling of one profession was not for me at an early age, and I carried that passion for exploration of all of life with me along my travels. I have my own business that is part accounting, part counseling, part education, and part crafts, but all things that I love. I am using my gifts for service to a greater good, for serving to a God who completely loves me. Best yet, I have learned my lessons of my past to propel me forward and to pay it forward to others who are still imprisoned with their mind's stories.

Have you ever read a biography and marveled at the amount of research done on someone's life? If you really want a treat to learn thoroughly about someone's life, check out anything by Dr. Elliott Engel. He is a magical speaker who dedicates exactly one hour to a focused subject, usually a famous author. The amount of details you learn from his rich stories is unfathomable. I have been fortunate to hear so many of his stories through speaking engagements, recorded material, and books that I have many talks thoroughly memorized. Ask me something about Charles Dickens. (Dr. Engel's primary studies began with Charles Dickens.) Go ahead – anything. I mention Dr. Engel's thoroughness because this is how much research you should do about your own life, your own autobiography.

When you need to see a doctor, they first listen to your symptoms. Based on what you say, the doctor then wants to run some tests. The data from the tests then dictates what you need. This is the exact same process for therapists. Data needs to be collected. I have a series of worksheets that I like to use to help me to know your world when I am coaching.

Lately, I have been exposed personally to a large variety of personality tests that are windows into what makes me tick. By exposing myself to a variety of tests, I have been able to zero in on how my brain works, where I am more likely to gravitate, why I should show myself forgiveness, and what labels to discard. One of the biggest labels I think by which many people feel threatened is being lazy. It is so easy to just call ourselves lazy than by looking at why we are doing some work over other work.

Personality tests help us to see that there is so much more going on than just laziness. For example, carving out time to write this book is no big deal for me. I rarely procrastinate on my set writing time. However, the laundry in my home is quite another matter. Whenever I am collecting, loading, unloading, folding, or putting away laundry, lots of negativity on my worth bubble up in my mind. Personality tests did not teach me about how much I hate laundry, but they did open my eyes to the complexity of the brain and our responses to our thoughts. Our actions have everything to do with how we think and have thought about everything.

One of my latest obsessions is with Gallup's Strengths Awareness. Gallup (yes, the same company who does the polls) and Dr. Don Clifton developed thirty-four different strengths. We all possess these strengths to a varying degree, but our top five strengths speak to how we typically function. When I first took the test, I immediately rolled my eyes because RESPONSIBILITY was my #1, top dog strength. Ugh. I rolled my eyes because I already knew way before the test that I have a dysfunctional relationship with responsibility by taking on others' problems. When I met with a Strengths Coach though, I discovered this fascinating concept that there are SHADOWS to our strengths.

Ooooooooh, now we are getting somewhere. When I looked up the shadow side of responsibility, I found: "Micromanager, obsessive, can't say no, and takes on too much."
https://www.med.umn.edu/sites/med.umn.edu/files/strengths_quick_refer ence_guide_w_pro_con_.pdf

Yes, that perfectly sums up how I feel ALL THE TIME. Or, should I say that is how I FELT! Yes, I have learned, through lots of introspection and soul-searching, to drop Responsibility down to the #4 strength. Yes, I still over-commit, but just knowing my tendencies to over-commit, I have shown myself more grace. I stopped labeling myself with the countless negative adjectives playing like a record in my mind, and I set out on a journey to stop focusing on feeling responsible for others' problems. By being more aware of my tendencies, I have learned that there really is a lack of boundaries in my life. It felt like a doctor had finally diagnosed my condition correctly, but the doctor here is a personality test.

Try to take as many personality tests as you wish. Unfortunately, what I have found is that many people cling to the results of just one test. They think that is how their personality was, is, and will be forever. Remember that I took the test later and dropped responsibility down to #4. You too can change what you do not like.

It was not until I was doing my own self-exploration that I uncovered my dysfunctional relationship to work. My father's philosophy was that if you were taking someone else's money, you gave 100% the entire time. Plus, if you were having fun while you were working, you were doing it wrong. These sound like practical, responsible tips for an employee. But, for someone who followed all rules to the nth degree, it was a death sentence. I became a robot and completely neglected myself as an employee who had a unique contribution. I saw my value strictly in terms of whether I was following the rules, and I put zero uniqueness into my work. Even as I write this now, I did not fully realize the ramifications of this strict belief that work cannot be fun.

When you find out all about yourself, it is important information because it can be a road map on how you would like to improve. When you see something that you do not like about yourself, now you know what you would like to change. Remember from Part 1 where I described how Dave Ramsey likes to clap his hands to just change. While I wish it were as easy as clapping your hands twice, it is a great reminder that we usually make change much more complicated than it has to be. Personality tests help map out a direction for being more of who you want to be. If you know me, you know I love to laugh. If you live three towns away, odds are you've heard my laugh. With only forty-three girls in my Senior high school class, there were plenty of traditional awards to distribute. We had our Most Likely to Succeed, First to Likely Get Married, Most Beautiful, etc. What was my award? I received the lesser known Most Able to Entertain Herself in a Closet Alone award. But, you know what? It's entirely true.

As described earlier in the book, I have this "condition" of getting laughing fits. Give me a minute as I recall a funny scenario from my past, and I will start to laugh uncontrollably. I've tried to tone down my laugh, my father has desperately tried, and yet it is what it is. It's not for attention; my laugh and I have been together in good, funny times and in the bad times. So, having the rule that I was not allowed to laugh at work made me split into two faces of Ead (my father's nickname for me). I was one person at work and another everywhere else. This, too, does not sound too bad, and it sounds very professional. But, like most things with me, a rule is a rule, and I carried it way too far. I then felt guilty (not like a regular kind of guilty but an Edie OCD kind of guilty) whenever I was enjoying any aspect of work. This then turned into a ritual of punishing myself for doing work that I enjoyed. If there was part of my job I enjoyed, I put it off and tried to do work not only that I hated but work where I lacked ability.

For example, I went into the field of social work to work with stroke patients and their families. My grandfather's stroke and the lack of familiar support that I experienced motivated me to help families. My first job out of my Master of Social Work degree was in the physical rehabilitation unit of a hospital. Most of the patients had suffered strokes, and I was working with the patients and their families. Voila! This was my perfect job. But, in addition to this unit, I was also the social worker for a regular medical ward of the hospital. This was a unit where patients were suffering from all variety of medical issues.

Many sufferers of COPD (Chronic Obstructive Pulmonary Disease) were on this unit, and this was a particularly difficult diagnosis for me. I just could not stomach the gurgling sounds with breathing. For the most part though, these COPD patients had ample familial support and did not need my services. Where did I usually work? Yes, I punished myself for not wanting to work with COPD patients and preferring stroke patients that I usually worked the regular medical unit. Even though I was better at my job on the rehab floor where I was needed more, I felt I was not supposed to be enjoying my experience. The COPD patients did not even need me, but I had a knack for punishing myself.

I bring up this example to show you that I never put two and two together. Until I became obsessive with understanding how I tick, I did not know about this self-inflicted, dysfunctional punishment. And, this is why this book definitely belongs in the self-help section. I am helping myself. I did not realize that this is all done by ME until I wrote this chapter. I continued to blame my father for the obsessive work torture I gave myself. By typing out this example, I can more clearly see that it is great news that the problem resides with my thoughts. This means that the solution to the problem resides with me too. At some point in life, you realize it is not really about the circumstances in your life but how you processed those circumstances. That is fabulous news though because the solution now is in your control.

When you realize that your history with your parents and your family shaped who you are, you also realize that your perceptions can be changed. You have zero excuse to not change. It would be much easier to go through life blaming others for your situation. But, if you put in the work to find a better way, you start driving the car. Most anxiety arises when you feel you are not in control. By becoming obsessive about learning what makes you tick, you can find where you need to work. You are in the driver's seat on your life. You are in control.

DEFINE

Top Adjectives

Learning as much as you can about yourself is a continuous process. After all, your past continues to grow as you age. Hopefully after completing step one of the four step process, you understand your childhood better and what experiences are still very alive for you, currently and still. Now, step two involves finding some treasures from your past. Let's summarize your childhood into themes, and let's describe our summaries with adjectives.

Please write down the top three NEGATIVE adjectives to describe your childhood. What are the top three that come to mind first? The most immediate answers are usually the purest. Yes, my focus is usually on the positive when I work, but in this case, it is important to spend some time with negative adjectives that describe your childhood. If one or a few incidents from your childhood were particularly negative, note those. For example, if you suffered any kind of abuse but your family did not believe you or support you, all your adjectives may be from that one incident. If you had a general feeling from childhood that was less than positive, that feeling will probably be in your top three. Whatever adjectives you choose, you have complete freedom here to choose YOUR adjectives. There is no judgment on what you think you should choose or if it represents what others' reality was in your family. Choose what is the most real for you.

Next, I'd like you to return to the exercise earlier in the book when you defined your top, #1 problem. Do you remember what that was? Do you see any connection to your top problem and the negative adjectives from your childhood? Does your resolution of how to solve your current, top problem possibly have anything to do with coming to terms with what you still need from childhood?

Try to find the connections between your top, current problems and the meaning you've given to past, painful experiences. For example, you might have suffered from loneliness in childhood and concluded that you aren't worthy of being an equal participant at social gatherings. You may have made conclusions about yourself and what you lack based on your childhood experiences. Have you personalized labels and negative adjectives from your past that are still affecting your interactions today? How have you made sense of the world based upon your past? What meaning did you give to the world based on your experiences? How did you personalize traumatic events? Do you blame yourself for unfortunate events in the past? Does it now make sense why I am called the Queen of Questions? Once you see a connection to your past, you are really peeling back the layers. You are closer to solving the real problems.

You can change the assumptions you made about yourself by refuting and changing the conclusions you made so long ago about life and about your part in the past. Do you ever sometimes worry that you've married the spitting image of one of your parents? Do you ever feel like you are trying to resolve something from the past with a current situation? I see clients every day where they are trying to solve problems from the past with current people. Let me save you some agony. If you are trying to solve your past problem with a current situation, you will always feel you have fallen short. The resolution will likely never feel

107

enough. That is the bad news. The good news is that you can solve the problem of the past by changing the meaning you have given to that past.

For example, once I examined how lonely I felt in childhood, I realized that even back then I was sick and tired of feeling lonely. I took action even back then. I was the only girl in the family, and I had my own, large bedroom. I felt pain at my Dad not wanting me to be seen or heard, but I retreated to my bedroom. I created a sanctuary and a fantasy world in my room that never made me bored. I rearranged furniture whenever I felt the desire, I listened to music, I made up stories, I sang and danced, and I loved every minute of it. In fact, alone time at my home now feels like time in my sanctuary all over again. Without feeling isolated, I never would have known the joy of being by myself. I know grown women who cannot be alone at all. There was a good purpose that was birthed from a deep pain. Without that loneliness, I may never have known the joy of solitude.

Now it's your turn. What sense did you make from your pain? How did your definition of yourself and the world change from what your pain taught you? Did you develop skills to cope with your pain? If you can let go of placing blame for your pain onto others or yourself, you can start to see your experiences differently. There are many examples where you will not be able to find any good from your very painful experiences, and that is definitely okay. Right now, I'm just asking that you see some connections to the problems of today and the pains from long ago. This is very much like a zillion pieced puzzle. This is tough stuff but very enlightening too.

Now for the best part, please list the top three POSITIVE adjectives from your childhood. (They do not have to be restricted to adjectives, but adjectives are so descriptive. Just note your top three positive words from childhood.) These three plus any other positive feelings are your road map to solving your current problems. This is where you have been trained to excel. Your current problems are likely most solvable by using your natural tendencies. You have been taught some positive skills to take with you in life.

For example, people who have lived childhoods filled with abuse and chaos typically are excellent readers of situations and of people. To survive times of chaos, skills at reading people's moods and triggers had to be developed. They are typically excellent judges of character and assessors of dangerous situations. They may not even be aware of how much they "know," but they know interpersonal communications on an unconscious level. It is very difficult to formally educate people to be good judges of character, but some people have had a whole childhood of training. Street smarts is another example of knowing through experience. While one may prefer that they never had to experience those hard knocks, nevertheless they have skills of which they might not even be aware.

So, the negative adjectives from the past help one to peel back the layers and start to solve the real issues. The positive adjectives from the past are the guides to how you will solve those problems.

Values

Being truly clear about your values helps solidify boundaries. People who suffer with anxiety typically have trouble with sticking to boundaries. When you are not clear about what you value, it is easy to compromise with yourself. Hopefully too, your values dictate all behaviors, including how you spend money.

What are your top four values in life? I recently heard a speaker say that it is imperative to have your top seven values well defined and front and center in your life. Let's start with your top four values. What is important to you? What qualities are important in your friendships, in your partner, in your work, etc.? What qualities do you feel are the most important to instill in children? By which qualities do you most want to be remembered?

Now that you have your top four, are you able to rank those four? Do you have a top value that trumps the others? I have counseled people where their top values have been at odds with each other. If honesty is one of your top four values as well as kindness, what happens if you are in a situation where you feel you must make a choice between being kind or being honest? I know many who have family as one of their very top priorities. But, what happens when family members become abusive? What happens if you must decide about breaking a promise of silence you made to your child in order to warn a parent about their child's dangerous choices? What is most important to you?

I clearly remember once being in an airport in South America, and my Dad turned to me for advice. He asked what was more valuable as he just witnessed a young boy pickpocket a man's wallet. There were plenty of police nearby, the man was out his wallet, and yet the boy looked very impoverished. I had no answer for my Dad. I too was frozen. It is better to rank your values now because you may be faced with a difficult dilemma that might call for an immediate decision.

Red Flags

> *"It's so clear now. It was not clear back then though. That's the good news and bad news... There are red flags, but they are kind of blurry, and they just zip on by."*
> — Paula Poundstone

What is a red flag? It is an indication to everyone that there is danger. Once we know our red flags have been raised, that is our signal to take extra good care of ourselves until we have removed ourselves from danger. It is a reminder that we feel weakened. Like out of sight is out of mind, we have a more difficult time of keeping our insecurities at bay when we are in a red flag situation.

If you can identify around four to five red flag zones, you generally will feel more aware when you have entered dangerous terrain. If you have numerous pet peeves, look for similar themes or adjectives. If you have way too many pet peeves and themes, it might be time to look at getting some assistance with processing your feelings. It may be that you are stuck in habits of seeing yourself as a victim in this world. If you find yourself angry all the time for any variety of circumstances, life becomes one big red flag. If you find yourself triggered at everything, it may indicate a lack of self-awareness.

Think of your red flags as warning signals like a fever is a warning sign of infection. We usually numb the fever by taking medicine, and while that provides relief, we need to figure out where the fever is guiding us. Our red flags are indications that there is danger. When your red flag is raised, it is an indication to either change your environment or change the impact someone has on you. You create distance between someone else's actions and your reactions! There is the power.

If you are not happy with the situation, change the setting, or change your thoughts about the situation. Once I was at my son's hockey game and had picked out a prime seat before the game. Right before the game started, a woman stood right in front of me. I mean RIGHT in front of me, and she never looked back to see if she was blocking anyone. It was like I "didn't exist." Uh-oh, you know now what that triggers in me. I was fuming the entire first period of the game. I could not let it go. All it would have taken was for me to move seats, but I was there first. (Yes, I heard the lack of maturity.) I was definitely not present for my child or myself. I could not tell you the score, let alone how well my son played. I was only focused on the selfishness of this woman and her audacity at not even seeing me. I was invisible to her, and yet my game watching experience was being ruined BY MY OWN MIND'S THOUGHTS.

As most distractions for me start with food, my husband bought me a pretzel after the first period. I completely forgot about the woman. She had not moved an inch, but my perspective shifted. Her selfishness was no longer the focus, and I was a happy camper. Nothing about the actual circumstances had changed, but my thinking had completely changed. I put the importance of someone's selfishness in its proper place. I realized that if I was that uncomfortable, all I had to do was move. I could change my situation, or I could remain stubborn to let someone else keep me in my mindset. Her selfishness was her problem, but I made it my problem. At the end of the game, I realized how different the first period felt compared to the next two periods.

Our thinking can be the problem or the solution.

The Zen story of the monks' journey relates to this concept. Many monks were traveling through rough terrain. They had taken vows of silence and zero physical touch while on this journey. When they came to a fast-flowing stream (almost river), there was a beautiful woman stranded and unable to pass to the other side of the rough waters. One monk motioned for her to get onto his back, and he carried her across the water. The other monks watched with astonishment but soon also crossed the stream themselves. At their final destination many hours later, one monk shouted the group's dismay at the audacity of the other monk breaking his vows. The monk's response was, "I put her down at the other side of the stream, but you have been carrying her the rest of the way." Others' problems can quickly become our problem. And, if you are used to carrying others' issues, the boundary between what is yours vs theirs becomes very, very thin. Is how you see the problem not working for you? Change your thinking.

Chapter Twenty-Eight: Trust and Tell

TRUST

By now, you have been taking your internal temperature, measuring how you feel about many different areas. You have learned how to show yourself grace, self-forgiveness, and kindness. By learning how to be good to yourself, you are proving to yourself that you can be trusted. The high value that you place on your word and fulfilling promises will equate to keeping promises to yourself.

Your feelings, thoughts, and instincts not only matter, but they can be relied upon as very valuable information. Honoring yourself as a welcomed visitor to the party of life means that you will be celebrating your uniqueness. Your strengths and talents are to be used for YOUR mission and purposes in life. By focusing less on others' paths and journeys, you will be able to gather the tools you need for your journey.

Compromises with yourself slowly whittle away trusting yourself. That is a wonderful argument to ease back on perfectionism and such extreme self-expectations that are unattainable. Every time you do not meet these high standards, you are trusting yourself less and less with showing up for yourself in healthy ways. Usually, people do not lie and cheat suddenly out of the blue. There are daily examples of trust breaks that have been building. It is so important to make small steps of building back trust. Show up for yourself in smaller ways to prove you can be trusted.

Trust yourself, and trust the process.

TELL

The truth sets you free, and freedom to be myself is one of my top values in life. Even if the facts of your past have suddenly been discovered, what remains consistent is your story as you know it. Adults have found out wild details about their childhoods later in life, like being adopted or having a twin, but your reactions and impressions can only be changed by you if you wish. No one else can take those realities from you; your impressions are yours.

One of the biggest crimes with lying to children is that they learn to not trust their own observations. When trusted adults are telling children lies, the children distrust their own vision. The angriest I have been in life has been when I did not trust my own observations. I believed the person and their story, despite what my observations were telling me.

I have been a public accountant and auditor. Thank goodness due diligence in the auditing world means that auditors must find substantial verification of people's stories. The numbers have to prove the explanations. If it does not make sense by the numbers, it is likely a lie. Unfortunately, there are not those checks and balances in the real world, and finding the lies can be trickier.

Despite what Jack Nicholson's character in A Few Good Men says, you actually can handle the truth. Lying to spare another's feelings rarely works in the long run. We are a lot more resilient when there is trust.

Most of my clients engage in Monday Morning Quarterbacking's mind tricks. Everyone has times of assigning self-blame for past decisions when we look back in time. We all have times when we second guess our decisions, but that is not showing our past selves grace because we already know the outcome when we look back in time. Comparing your decisions back then against a backdrop of knowing the outcome forces you to judge your past self so harshly. No one can compare a decision where the outcome is known to the agony of weighing and deciding different options. Remember these look backs in time are very one-sided; the brain discounts all of the effort put into past decisions. Credit is rarely given to your past self. It is unfair to your peace of mind and makes letting go almost impossible.

Tell the truth to yourself and to others. Always default to the truth. The truth is easy because you do not have to worry about how well you know all the details. You know what you know. Lies are messy and complicated. The more you lie, the more difficult the path is to follow, even for your own mind. You are not blaming anyone when you are telling the truth, not even finding fault with yourself. The truth just is what it is.

I consider myself a Truth Detective. This is not from a place of judgment; instead, it is from a place of knowing the freedom of the truth. Any time I hear one of my clients say, "I just wanted them to think I am … (insert an adjective)," I know they are trying to play themselves off as other than they naturally are. They are trying to be someone else. They are building up that fake persona, that outer layer that is hiding who they really fear they are on the inside. By continuing to create an outer persona, there is less freedom to be yourself.

Playing yourself off as smarter than you are is not sustainable. Acting differently while dating is not sustainable. Plus, the mental energy is exhausting to keep up pretenses. Of course, it is always good to put your best foot forward. But, if you feel your true nature needs to remain hidden, you will likely always be looking over your shoulder not for when you'll be found out as incompetent but when you'll be found out as untrustworthy.

There are no white lies in my book either. Big lies do not usually come up out of the blue; usually, there have been build-ups of compromises with the truth. "I'm on the freeway right now" when you have not left the office yet is a lie where it might not seem to be causing harm. The more times that you are separating reality from what you say, the more your brain stops trusting you.

Any discussion on telling the truth must also include the addiction of gossip. The whole nature of pitting people against each other by gossiping creates a tornado of falsehoods. Have the rule that whatever you say about someone could just as easily be said if they were right next to you. It is certainly understandable that we have conflicts with people that are difficult to address directly to them. However, true resolution cannot function in a gossipy, petty world.

There is so much about life that is very difficult to explain. When we lie, we are arrogantly thinking we know how life can work to our advantage by manipulating it. By telling the truth to ourselves and others, we are freeing ourselves to be true to ALL of us, to love others too where they are at this moment, to build up people who feel broken, and to use our uniqueness as points of strength. Denying parts of ourselves means that we only accept the good qualities. Until we can embrace who we truly are, there is little chance of getting out of judgment to live freely. We can handle the truth to be FREE.

Chapter Twenty-Nine: Value, and Let Go

VALUE

"Freeing and relieved" are the most common words I hear when I ask my clients to describe their boost in self-worth. This boost is due to learning their self-value is in who the ARE and not in what they DO for others. Most ironically, when the focus is on their self-worth being in their very nature, what they do for others improves.

Resentment and bitterness are the natural by-products of continuing to serve out of obligation. While it feels like you are resenting the person to whom you are giving so much, it is more accurately resentment that you do not feel free to be yourself, your authentic and true self, to others.

When we give gifts of ourselves (mostly our time and energy but also material gifts) out of a sense of obligation or a sense of expectation for something in return, it is not a true gift. Gifts with future price tags of expected reciprocation are the worst kinds of gifts to give or to receive. When you give to get and you do not receive anything back in return, there is a trail of destruction from the gift. It would be better to not give at all than to give a gift expecting anything in return.

The comedian Michael Jr. explains the concept of natural gifts perfectly. Most people have the most difficulty with receiving gifts of any kind – words of praise and any form of help in particular. When my clients describe a deep need to help people, my first investigation is if they are giving naturally or more out of an obligation. Many times, our gifts to others are to guarantee a return of love and acceptance in some form. The gift is usually wrapped in disguise of being in people pleasing mode. These gifts with loaded expectations are not from our natural

117

zone. We are placing higher value on our self-worth through what we do for others.

The best biblical justification for taking our natural talents to show the magnificence of our Father is the story of the three servants. As each servant was given different talents, the two who multiplied their talents received their rewards. We are given natural gifts from God, and it is up to us to develop these talents. We keep refining our abilities, sharpening our saws, and strengthening our muscles. As we grow each day, we naturally give these talents to others as testimony of God's goodness. But, when we give with expectations for return of these gifts, we are not honoring God's beautiful talents given uniquely to us.

For parents, showing how you value your children for whom they are instead of what they do will be walking the talk. If we are stuck valuing ourselves merely in what we do for others, start practicing by valuing others for whom they are. Most children hear only their parents' words on how to be better. This focus on how well the children perform can lead children to think they are only valuable when they perform well. This applies really to anyone who wants to inspire others to be free to be themselves. If you aren't yet convinced you can give yourself the freedom of valuing who you are, give the gift to another person. Soon, you will feel how relieved that child or person is, knowing you love them no matter what. At the end of the day, I guess we all are trying to give each other the gift God has been giving us all along – unconditional love.

Most friction in the workplace comes either when we try to perform like robots to complete our workload or when we compare our work to others. Companies do not hire robots. For most professions, you were hired to do a job because of your unique skills and attributes. Remember that the servants in the parable were given a different number of talents. They were rewarded when they multiplied based on what they were given and not based by the highest number of talents made. We too will be asked on how we were responsible for what we were given.

Celebrate your uniqueness in your offering of service to others. Give without the expectation of a return. You will be valuing yourself by your unique nature, your gifts from God.

LET GO

The most difficult of the ten ingredients to resolve is a Heightened Sense of Responsibility, and the most difficult of the eight verbs in this four-step process is the ability to let go. Of what are you letting go? You are learning how to be responsible solely for what is in your control. I am way ahead of you on this one. "But, I am a control freak and like to be in control of everything at all times. Does that mean I get don't have to let go?" Good try, but this step involves learning how to be in your lane alone and not to assume control of anyone else's problems.

"But, I love to help people." That too is code for this innate desire to control your environment in order for life to work the way you want and for you to feel less vulnerable to your fears and worst-case scenarios. When you feel called to be the FIXER OF EVERYTHING, it is not a badge of honor but a deeply painful place of feeling responsible for everyone's pain.

As much as you love your family and friends, accepting responsibility for their pain is robbing them of the growth that they could have experienced from taking responsibility of their own, unique pain. Remember that I believe our pain is our greatest opportunities to be catapulted to greater growth. Absorbing another's pain is not a badge of honor, but it keeps you from addressing your own unique lessons.

If you would not take the credit, you cannot also take the blame. I know when I am in a danger zone of feeling responsible outside my zone when I expect superhero strength from myself. When I would have to be God-like in order to fix another's situation, I am outside of my zone. I was able to let go of my greatest pain once I heard how superhuman I would have to be to accept blame for another's situation. I did not want to think of myself as God-like, and so it was much easier to let go.

These superhero expectations usually happen when we look back in time or become a Monday morning quarterback. It is such an unfair mental exercise to compare what we decided back then to our look backs when we already know the outcome. Our minds were in protection mode back then with the information we had at that time. Being exceptionally kind to our past self means that we can let go of second guessing past decisions.

Through many of the processes described in this book, you have learned to see pain as a window of opportunity. Your gut instincts, your feelings, and your thoughts are also signs to pay attention to what needs addressing for you and you alone. It can be exceedingly difficult to realize the depth of how much responsibility you have absorbed for others' areas. Through reshaping your emotional reactions from painful stories of your past though, you are beginning to learn your own unique lessons. By letting go and letting God, you are staying in your natural zone of uniqueness. Take your strengths, your pain, your red flags, and your values to carve the best path possible. Stay on your road, and you will be role modeling others to stay in their lanes and let go. You've got this!

Chapter Thirty: Write, and Change

WRITE THE BACK STORY

Now that you have your list of adjectives, values, and red flags, it is time to write the story of your past. Your three negative adjectives are the missing ingredients from your past. Those three negative adjectives represent what was missing in your life that created great longing. The three positive adjectives represent your strengths to get you to what you have been missing. Your values guide you through unchartered territories. Your red flags show you the obstacles along the way.

Brene Brown describes the connection between our impressions and our thoughts with one question: What story are you telling yourself? In an interview with Oprah Winfrey, Brene explains her mind's story if Oprah were to ignore a compliment Brene had given on how well the interview had gone. Brene would immediately create the story that Oprah must not like her. Brene's default assumption would be to assume Brene was not enough. The actual facts of the story would be that Oprah did not hear Brene's comment. Should Oprah then be held responsible for the story that Brene created? Of course not, but how many times do we blame others for the stories we have created in our own minds? How many times do our default insecurities create an alternate reality?

I have blamed a lot of people for my loneliness. I now know that I had to go through repeated examples of being shunned to learn the lesson that my value as a human is not equated with being invited to a party or asked to join a group. My self-worth should never be dependent on who likes me, but oh my, it certainly has been a key ingredient to my value. After all, I firmly believe I am a child of God. You are a child of God. Everyone on this earth is a child molded out of God's image. That alone should prove our self-worth. How silly it sounds that my self-worth has been so fragile that it could be decimated by not being included in a party invitation. How often is your self-worth decimated by something outside of your control? How can you stop blaming others for your mind's stories?

With many of my lessons learned, I hope to now pay it forward by teaching people to first learn their back story. Discover the negative language you have been using to tell your history. This is very emotional work, but the exceptionally good news about this work is that it is all under your control. When we blame others for our circumstances, we are relinquishing control to someone else. As people with anxiety love control, do not relinquish your history to others. You can gain control for your life by changing the thoughts that you have told yourself repeatedly over time.

Tell your back story. Write your back story. It is not just the facts that are important but describe how those facts had an impact on you. You must first tell all the subtle nuances of the story before you can learn to change your story. Once you understand your story, you can zero in on what you need now as an adult.

Ultimately, your back story should be one small paragraph of four to five sentences. To begin though, you will need one to two pieces of paper. List everything about your childhood that is relevant to the person you are today. I am calling childhood up until eighteen years of age, but if something very impactful happened after childhood, of course you can add that too. Include anything that comes to mind, even if you are not sure it makes any sense. Remember that you are writing how events affected YOU, not just the facts of the situation. Before you begin though, there is a major ground rule.

Everything you include should be only in terms of how you processed the facts. Blaming others should not be part of the exercise.

For example, instead of saying that when your parents divorced your mother blamed you for the divorce, you could rephrase the facts by saying that you felt responsible for the failure of your parents' marriage and for your dad leaving the family. Just because a parent blames a child for something does not automatically mean that the child assumes and internalizes that blame. (It is usually the case though.) Do you see the difference? Instead of explaining the facts of the story, you are telling descriptively how you internalized those facts. The important part of the story is not that the mother blamed the child but that the child accepted the responsibility for something outside of his/her control.

The reason your story needs to be told in terms of how you internalized circumstances is because you are wording the problem where the solution is under your sole control. You are not changing the facts of the story, but you will be working on changing how you processed internally those facts. Remember too that what you write should be relevant to the you of today. If there were momentous events that do not have a particular impact on who you are today, you don't need to include them. But, if you are not sure, please include them. It is much more likely that you are not even aware of the impact of how you have processed certain life events. These are hard-wired associations that live in the subconscious mind.

Make the details very personal with as many descriptive adjectives as possible. Whenever possible, note the meaning you gave to certain life events, if you know them. Some meanings may become clear as you are writing down the details. With the example of a divorce, you might describe how you personalized the divorce being related to how ill you were as a child and how you felt the divorce was your fault. When you hear of celebrities writing their autobiographies, they describe the process as painful but also cathartic. You will likely be making connections and uncovering meanings that you never realized existed.

Please put that list away for a bit of time. If other items arise in your mind that you would like to include, that is fine to add them to your papers. Have a few days of distance with your pages.

Be good to yourself here, and make sure that you have a support system because tough memories may resurface. Make sure you are in a healthy state of mind where you can handle this look back in time. Most of these memories are stored in your subconscious as a protective measure of the mind. This is emotional work reliving painful times. Especially when it becomes very painful, try to be a third-party narrator describing the scene as just an observer and not a participant.

After a bit of distance with your story, sharpen that pencil because you are going to start whittling. Take a large note card, and write down a few key words from some of the stories that you have listed. You are looking for patterns and themes from your stories. For example, my stories of the past have a quite common theme of an inability to let go. The idea here is to whittle down the story enough to be told in just four to five sentences. Pretend that your story is compacted into one suitcase on a trip. You might start out with lots of bags, but you can only take with you one piece of luggage.

WRITE THE FUTURE STORY

Once you have your back story in a compact paragraph, it is time to write your future story. I know this is also quite emotional, but if you are able to do so, pretend you are writing your own obituary. I recently lost my 90+ year old aunt, and she had actually prepared her own obituary. It does not need to be a story that others see, but include all of what you hope your life has been. Include dreams and goals that still might be feasible. Obviously, it does not do much good to list dreams that cannot physically happen, but try to include stretches of goals that still are possible.

Many, many people limit how they describe their dreams in terms of what they see as possible. I am asking you to note what you desperately want EVEN IF you do not see the way it can happen. After all, isn't that what faith is, believing in something we cannot see? Most of us deny what we want because we do not want to get our hopes up. If you do not have your desires front and center, how can you ever fulfill them? Can you win the lottery when you do not buy a ticket? Focus less on the how and more on the what.

In other words, try not to filter your story by only including goals that you believe are reachable. As Les Brown says, "Shoot for the moon, and if you miss, you will still be among the stars." If you have wanted to be a famous rock star, you could still include in your future story how you sang and entertained many with your singing. Have fun with your story because life should be fun. Do not be limited by what you think is only still possible. Dream.

> *"They make glue out of horses. I don't know how they started that. Who saw that potential? Were they working in a stationery store when a horse walk by? 'Hey, wait a minute. Wait a minute. I think he could be glue. Leave that to me to pick out the really sticky ones. See that horse over there that's weaving around all over the place? I think he's out of his mind. He'll be crazy glue.'"*
> — Jerry Seinfeld

CHANGE

Now comes the really focused part. Take your back story, and place it next to your future story. Have your list of negative and positive adjectives, your red flags, and your values around these two stories for your review. You are now beginning the decluttering phase.

Where can you change your lenses on how you have processed your story? Where can you let go? What labels were you given that are no longer working for you? Free yourself.

I offer a serious note of caution here. I call it the dangers of the SWING OF THE PENDULUM. When we try to make a change, we usually go to the opposite extreme first. I have worked with many clients who have made severe changes in their lives from one extreme to another in hopes of coming to a point of balance. If one area of your life has become an addiction or obsession, usually the pendulum swings to the other extreme. As one addiction is lost, usually there is a replacement. Hopefully, the new obsession or addiction is not to the other extreme. In trying to course correct in life, we usually do not get it perfect the first time, and we have to experiment in order to find a method that works for us. For example, if one has not exercised much at all, going to an extreme exercise pattern will not likely be sustainable. If you were on a diet of only liquids, that is the swing of the pendulum for your metabolism, but eventually you will have to eat solid foods again. It might be what you need while you are making the changes, but eventually you will need to swing back enough to find your equilibrium.

Once you complete this book, you will have learned a lot about self-parenting, boundaries, and staying focused in the areas under your control. Change your back story enough for you to manifest your future story. After you finish learning about the many ways anxiety creeps into your life, you will know how to shed the chains that continue to bind you to the dysfunctional parts of your story.

As you are working on the stories of your past and the answers to the lists at the end of this chapter, the issues will change. That is good because it shows you are healing from the pain. As this is very much like peeling an onion, different layers are peeled as you are ready. Trust the timing. Of course, you know I have to remind you again. You also have to show yourself two things here - grace and self-forgiveness. This is not an easy process by any means. Fear of the unknown, which is where you are exploring, is powerful. Self-defenses have protected you fiercely to not peel back those layers. You have to be exceptionally good to yourself here. It is no longer working to beat yourself up. Labeling yourself as the problem is no longer protecting yourself.

Set yourself free from pain by learning to love who you are.

Top Three Adjectives to Describe Childhood:

1.
2.
3.

Top Three Ingredients You Miss from Childhood:

1.
2.
3.

Four Top Red Flags:

1.
2.
3.
4.

Four Top Values (by order of importance if you can):

1.
2.

3.

4.

Your Top Five Strengths: You can come up with your own strengths, you can choose from Gallup's Strengths Finder list, or you can take the actual test.

1.

2.

3.

4.

5.

The Summary of Your Past (yes, there are only a few lines to give a condensed version where you only are giving the most important elements to YOUR story):

_____

_____

_____

_____

_____

_____

_____

_____

Your Future Story (describe your future story as if you are writing a short obituary for how you were known in this life):

_____

_____

_____

_____

_____
_____
_____
_____

Action Plan to Be Your Truest Self:

1.
2.
3.
4.
5.
6.

_____
_____
_____
_____
_____
_____
_____
_____
_____
_____
_____
_____

Chapter Thirty-One: Anxiety's Swear Words

I love clean comics/comedians. Jay Leno used to say that swearing during comedy is a crutch. It is a lower quality joke if it needs a swear word to be funny. If I keep my environment clean from constant profanity, it makes me feel better. This is the same theory to apply to anxiety. If we rid ourselves of the swear words that trigger anxiety or anxious thinking, we feel better. In addition to the previously described swear words of Perfect, Responsible, and Criticism, the following are more of Anxiety's Swear Words: Someday, Not Enough, What If, and Fault/Blame.

SOMEDAY

Especially with regards to hoarding tendencies on the anxiety spectrum, Someday is one of the worst of the swear words. (However, Perfection is right up there.) One of my favorite sayings is: Today Is Someday. I was reflecting for weeks on the beauty of this expression, and one day I was at a gas station and looked up to find a billboard. I could not believe it. A hospital's advertising said:

Translation is: Some day is today.

Today is someday. It can take fifteen years to become an overnight success. Someday thinking is procrastination for happiness. The distance in your mind between the present moment and achievement of your goals is a great clue into how much you will use today to advance in your goals. If you are constantly picturing your future self as very different from who you are today, the link is weak to realizing your dreams.

Thinking "Today is someday" means that you can do something toward your goals today. Whether it is a big step or a little really does not matter as much as it is a step forward. Action beats dreaming every time in the game of life. When our goals seem so far in the future, our daily steps do not seem to be relevant. Someday thinking is the child of procrastination and perfectionism. When you picture your fully realized, future self, the image seems perfect. Yet, the distance between how you picture yourself today as compared to that fully realized person gets farther and farther away. Try each day to identify what steps you took to advance toward that self-image. Shore up the distance between the you of today and the future you.

When I am debating with a few options on a daily basis, I try to picture myself waking up the next morning. Will I be happier or sadder the next morning with today's decision? If you only see today's action as a sacrifice, try to picture how you will see it tomorrow. Wouldn't it be great if we made today's decisions based on how we think we will feel about them tomorrow?

Someday thinking is particularly dangerous with financial planning. By NOT doing planning today for retirement, college, vacations, cars, emergencies, etc., we cannot recoup what we have already spent. Of course, all spending today cannot be for the future, but we are trying to shorten the gap in our thinking between our present and future selves.

NOT ENOUGH

The problem with feeling Not Enough is that Enough's finish line is constantly moving. Just when you think you have reached the pinnacle of accomplishment, you find another way you are lacking. Enough is a close cousin to perfection because when can either really be reached?

I usually know healing is occurring when I see clients are engaging in activities to be better instead of perfect. Better also has to do in comparison with themselves only. It is when we start the dreaded comparisons with others that proves to ourselves that we are Not Enough. If we are able to stay in our own lane and be better than our yesterdays, we are extending ourselves grace and self-forgiveness.

When I hear clients telling me their life stories, I am constantly reminding them that they are not showing themselves grace and self-forgiveness by describing themselves that way. Every time they look back on their pasts, they focus on what they have done wrong and rarely give themselves any credit. If this feels like you, let's learn about the brain's self-protection focus. Your brain is probably life's most complex asset, but really the brain's main focus is survival. Your mind is always looking for signs of danger in order to protect itself. That is why we find ourselves focused on what is wrong because the brain wants to avoid danger. But, the downside of seeing only the danger signs when we look back in time is that we usually only see the negative aspects of our past. We forget what we have done out of protection, the positive steps we took to survive. We rarely give our past selves credit.

A silly example of this is when I have lost some paperwork. I will tear the entire house apart looking for something that is lost, and the

132

last place I usually go is where that paper is supposed to be. Instead of going to the files, I assume that I have not filed my paperwork. When I find a lost item right where it was supposed to be, I realize yet again that I have not given my past self-credit.

One day I was watching a video on how this woman learned how to sew her own clothes. To me, sewing your own clothing is the ultimate proof that you can sew. It is very difficult to do. I was lamenting that I will probably never be a good seamstress to sew my own clothes. I was really criticizing myself at my lack of sewing ability. As I went to get dressed that morning with my head hung down in shame, I was looking through my closet for some clothes. One of the first items I touched was a skirt that yes, I had sewn myself years earlier. I recalled that every time I wear that fun skirt, I receive a compliment. I had completely forgotten that I had already taught myself the talent for which I longed. I gave myself zero credit that I had arrived long ago.

Where do you need to give yourself credit? Where do you find yourself lacking? Where are you still traveling and yet maybe you have not realized that you already arrived?

WHAT IF

Ah, What If... thinking. Whenever we engage in mind predictions of negative events, we usually forget our power. When we picture these dire possibilities happening, we forget that we have equipped ourselves with a strength through past experiences. We have already had some solid training to meet whatever comes our way. Usually, people do not finish their sentences when they engage in What If scenarios. The fear of the scenario keeps them from seeing what assets they bring to the painful scenario, what prior experiences have taught them already, and where they have already prepared.

Most anxiety stops us in our tracks. It paralyzes us from action. But, action is exactly what is necessary to combat the anxious thoughts. For example, let's say you are paralyzed with fear of thinking What If there is a huge earthquake. Finish out that scenario. Let's say there is a large earthquake, and you are at home. Do you have enough supplies to last you for quite awhile? Do you have batteries, a battery radio, enough water, and emergency contacts written down? If we are able to push past the fear that stops us, we can feel empowered that we are prepared enough for an emergency.

What If, stinkin' thinkin' negates one's power. These limiting fears fail to factor in the power and strength within us. Next time you find yourself in a tornado of What If thinking, finish the thoughts. Act like your own attorney representing yourself, and prove to your mind that you have what it takes to face any scenario that comes your way. Of course, faith is one of the most powerful tools for What If thinking. Faith in a higher being who gives us nothing more than what we can handle prevents us from feeling isolated and alone to tackle complicated situations. Faith is knowing that "it" has to happen this way in order for us to be propelled forward. There is a life lesson to be learned in every scenario, and it is our job to stay open to learning those lessons. We have been equipped with the right tools to learn whatever comes our way, but anxious thoughts are the first barrier to unleashing our power.

Finish every What If scenario with the thought, "Well, if that happens, I will figure it out then."

FAULT/BLAME

Did you do it "on purpose?" That is one of the first things that parents usually ask when something has gone wrong. It is really difficult for a child to understand and interpret intentions. For those who are hyper-sensitive, repeatedly asking them about their intentions can bring a lifetime of questioning their own motives. That is one of the main reasons I thought there was something deeply bad about myself. I kept questioning my motives and kept blaming myself when bad things happened. It was only until I faced a litany of my good intentions that I realized overall I was a good person who made mistakes and sometimes lashed out when I myself was hurt. There is a big difference between doing a bad act where you know you are hurting someone and feeling that your entire being is bad. By the way, you might be shocked to know how many people define themselves as all bad or at least fear they might be all bad. And, you thought you were the only one! (For more on our cognitive distortions, please check out the book called *Feeling Good* by Dr. David Burns.) Make sure you are not labeling yourself as all bad because it will be very difficult to show yourself grace and forgiveness.

Our minds process matters in order to bring logical meaning to the world. When something bad happens, it is easier to assign fault than to just chalk it up to fate. We have no control if we define life as just up to fate, but we have the illusion of control if we can assign blame. I work with so many people who would rather accept responsibility than to wait to see if the other person takes the reigns. "Oh, I'll just do it myself" is a quite common attitude because now we feel in total control over fate and over others doing it differently than how we want it done.

Next time you are quick to assign blame onto yourself or another, try to see it as an attempt to gain control. By acknowledging that you feel out of control and in such an uncomfortable zone, you are not blocking that energy. You are seeing the situation for what it is. When we assign blame, our focus is not on what we can learn from this situation. Most people think that the lesson they have learned is that they cannot rely on anyone. They add fuel to the fire of thinking that anything done right has to be done by them alone. By letting go of the need to control and by focusing on the opportunity to learn a valuable lesson, you will give energy to moving forward. While you might not have done something on purpose, your solution will be done with focused energy and good intention.

Chapter Thirty-Two: Listen

Have you ever walked out of a meeting with a colleague and then started discussing what happened in the meeting? At some point, did you wonder if you were in the same meeting as your colleague? That phenomena happens because you both bring your own personal issues, your history, your education, your baggage, your passions, and your interests to everything you attend. Your view is different from my view because where we focus is different.

I am currently a therapist with an online agency where we provide counseling services through posting (like email) or video and phone sessions. If I can rid myself of all that is blocking me from active listening, my clients will benefit. The traditional form of counseling with the counselor and the client in the same room at the same time is changing quickly. That is one of the main reasons why I wanted so desperately to counsel online; when I am reading what people post, I am not worried about how I will respond. When someone is telling me their story face-to-face, a good portion of my energy is taken away from the client and focused on how I will respond. My best work is when I am alone to create without anyone watching. I am able to listen purely.

What do you need to be able to listen to yourself? Do you play a lot of roles in life – mother/father, daughter/son, sister/brother, worker/colleague, and friend? Are you so focused on others' paths that you have lost your own? Have you been pushing down difficult feelings that are just too painful to confront? Do you numb pain? It is extremely easy to lose your way. It is extremely easy to forget your essence. How has pain affected your life? Do you feel bad, but you aren't sure why?

Our thoughts have been with us an exceptionally long time. Synapses have formed to create strong roads associating sights, smells, locations, and sounds to feelings. And, when the mind is faced with the unknown, the mind will choose what is known. The fear of the unknown blocks us from branching out even when the known patterns are very, very dysfunctional. Our "worst case scenarios" are usually something that has never happened to us because the fear of the unknown is just that frightening. I believe that is why people continue to put up with dysfunctional relationships and pain because the unknown feels so much more frightening.

Enter faith. If you have a baseline faith that God will take care of everything, it is much easier to break the dysfunctional patterns. The unknown may be scary, but if you know in the depths of your heart that God will take care of you, the unknown's power severely diminishes. If God and the devil were captains of a prison ball game, the devil's first choice on his team would be fear. Fear keeps you in the prison of your past.

Are you ready to take on the path less traveled? (Oh, the book *The Road Less Traveled* by Dr. M. Scott Peck is terrific!) What should you pack on your trip? A set of cleaned-out ears to hear and an open heart to show yourself grace are key ingredients. As you go through each day, be a spectator of your own life. Many of my clients ask if journaling will help. Yes, of course, journaling is a great activity, but my caution is that journaling should not take on a life of its own. Journaling alone does not solve the problem but, finding the patterns through journaling is the real work.

What are the important parts when you are a spectator in your own life? As soon as you sense a feeling coming into your mind/heart/soul, try to think about the thoughts you had right before the feeling. This is why I am going to create a line of travel journals. You need to write this stuff in your journal as close to when you are feeling the feelings. It is difficult to go back in time to re-create the possible thoughts that were going through your mind. I keep a notebook in my purse at all times. (I have OCD; there is a lot in my purse, but that is for a different book.) I am constantly writing down things that inspire me, quotes I read or hear, stories that make me feel, etc., but I don't like to engage in the activity of looking at my negative feelings. I have to push myself to look at this stuff because it's easier to deny its existence. But, that's exactly the kind of internal conflict that has gotten me into so much trouble in the past. When I see a disconnect between my thoughts and reality, I think the problem is with me. Now I realize the problem is still with me, but the answer is to break the association or disprove the life assumption, instead of just labeling myself negatively.

This is exactly why I became so enamored with stress management. The exact same stressor/event can occur within a company, but every employee will have a different reaction. Why one person reacts very negatively and another sees it as an opportunity says everything about their different pasts and thoughts about their pasts.

At an early age, the hard wiring of our minds began. As our brains were still developing, we processed our thoughts about events differently. Our past is entirely relevant because associations between seemingly unlike events, thoughts, and feelings were formed. We have become so familiar with these associations that we do not recognize their existence anymore.

I fully understand that this stuff is very difficult to bring back up and figure out again. But, if we are not willing to change how we think about an event, we are leaving matters in others' control. I know how much anxiety sufferers do not like to do that! Plus, denying the existence or impact of negativity causes physical as well as emotional pain. Sicknesses and diseases can develop when our immunities are down. Continually pushing down pain means that the energy has to go somewhere eventually.

I call the inability to deny the existence of negativity any longer WAWA. Anxiety sufferers usually develop Work Arounds (WA) for relieving the pain of anxiety. Do you have phobias related to germs? Maybe your Work Around becomes not shaking hands with anyone (Hello, Howie) or bringing your own bed linens when you travel. Do you have social anxiety? Maybe your Work Around is to grocery shop online to avoid people. When your Work Arounds (WA) don't Work Anymore (WA) you get WAWA. That is usually the point when people seek help for their anxiety. Think of a Work Around as medicine for an illness. When you have built up a tolerance in your system and the medicine is no longer working, you have to seek alternative treatment. This is usually what happens when one numbs pain with alcohol. When it takes more and more alcohol to feel numb, eventually they will likely have to address the problem of alcoholism or an addiction to numbing.

When you are in WAWA, the work is not to find another Work Around; the real work is to stop numbing the pain. If you can get to a point where you relinquish the need to numb, you will experience a freedom like no other. For a long time, there have been many secondary gains to not change the status quo. There are benefits to keeping your pain. This is a chapter on listening. Did you hear that line about benefits? Yes, the time is now to face the benefits of holding onto the anxiety. Until you learn how the so-called benefits are really deterrents to happiness, the anxiety will remain.

Chapter Thirty-Three: Self-Parenting

My dream is that every adult at some point in their life engages in the act of self-parenting. No matter how fabulous your childhood was, everyone has some inner child issues that are one's own responsibility to solve. Many clients I see for therapy are still desperately clinging to getting their childhoods "solved" or "fixed" by working with the actual people from their past. They still hold resentments, anger, bitterness, and blame for what happened. Forgiveness is very difficult, especially when there has been trauma as a little child.

Self-parenting is the process of letting go of your REACTION to pain. If you believe that what happens to you in life, especially in the formative years, is for your overall well-being, then it is easier to let go. Usually people who have suffered abuse have personalized their lack of self-worth deeply. As adults, they have lived for a long time with these labels of not deserving love. Shedding those labels takes lots of introspection and training. This is where faith in God and trusting Him can be your strongest tool. God formed you in His likeness and knows your value. Therapy is so much easier with people who have faith because they usually believe that they were formed in the image of God. They see God as the ultimate parent who gives us what our earthly parents maybe could not.

My two mid-life purchases have been an old convertible PT Cruiser and an even older RV. One has a CD player, and the other does not. I cannot put the top down in the RV, and I cannot take a shower in the convertible. Oh, how I love these two vehicles, but I love them for different things that they offer. I do not expect these fabulous purchases to do something they are not equipped to do. That is why we have to release some expectations we have of others and of ourselves.

You cannot squeeze blood from a turnip, no matter how hard you squeeze. In order to heal, you have to let go of expecting others to deliver what they cannot give. Once you are able to let go of expecting THEM to help you, you have the freedom to give yourself what you need. If you did not experience the right role models to be a good parent, search for role models now to help you. Change the people in your group. Start reading some books to show you good parenting or good leadership examples. Break the cycle of looking to others to solve your reactions to the world.

I am by no means minimizing the pain from abuse many have experienced and how difficult it is to get to a point of valuing one's self enough to self-parent. You have lived with pain for a very long time, and just showing up to heal might feel like you are releasing people from evil acts. This process of self-parenting is not acceptance of evil as good for your growth. It is acceptance of being valuable to heal fully. If others are not showing up how you need, your healing does not have to be on hold until they do show up. You did not deserve the abuse. You deserve to be made whole again, and you don't need to depend on anyone else for your healing.

When people are suffering from their pasts, to make sense of it, they have created images of others who have hurt them. Usually, their focus is on the trauma or abuse of others solely. When one focuses on only the negative actions of a bully, the bullies become larger than life in one's mind. Let's call these people "mind bullies." The mind bullies and the actual people become two separate beings. Self-parenting is giving oneself tender loving care to heal from the bullies in one's mind. Caution – the actual people may still be very harmful and need to be avoided. However, usually people get stuck to heal themselves because the actual bullies are not helping with the healing process. Self-parenting is so freeing because you do not need to hold the other person responsible for your own healing. No matter what has happened and who is not willing to help, you can set yourself free.

Chapter Thirty-Four: Even Though

Now that you have learned how important your back stories are to reshaping your emotional reactions to current issues, we can begin to go to the source of the problem. Emotional Freedom Technique (EFT) aka Tapping is an amazing energy tool to heal from your back stories.

EFT has the same philosophy as acupuncture but without the needles. EFT is acupressure. As we are learning more and more about the significant mind-body connection, we are learning about how energy can become blocked in us. Our bodies store unresolved issues, and EFT is a highly effective tool to release ourselves from blocked energy.

While EFT is an effective tool for therapists to work with clients on painful issues, EFT is also an amazing tool anyone can do themselves as down-regulation of emotions. Leave the very difficult stories of unresolved pasts to work with a trained therapist, but EFT is quite helpful to bring almost instant calmness and peace to your system.

After measuring yourself according to the Subjective Units of Distress Scale (SUDS) and through tapping on different meridians points as you go through a series of statements, you can gain a deeper understanding of your emotions. Just as essential oils, meditation, and prayer help with bringing peace through an almost hypnotic state, EFT also brings a depth to understanding your feelings and thought patterns from painful events. The beginning is the setup statement which is something along the lines of, "Even though I feel or think .... or ... happened, I deeply and completely love and accept myself." By acknowledging a negative emotion or thought, you are learning to accept all parts of yourself. This chapter is merely an introduction to the healing concept of Tapping to gain further permission to value all parts of yourself.

I initially was introduced to EFT when I attended a conference for entrepreneurs. At a reception the night before the conference, I approached a woman and asked her what she did for a living. She told me she was a Procrastination Coach. Right then, I knew why I had been called to attend the conference; I needed this coach! I enrolled in her coaching program where she explained that I could stop procrastinating by tapping on various parts of my body.

Thankfully, she had warned me before my first of six coaching sessions that I was going to feel exceptionally silly tapping on my body, especially after paying quite a lot of money to do so. I had one stated purpose for six sessions. Soon into the first session, we both realized I was there to heal a different and deeper wound from my past. I had an emotional issue that was essentially the root of many of my current problems. I had been dealing with this issue in one form or another for many, many years. I finished my EFT sessions with this coach and went on my merry way.

It was not until a year later that I realized basically this huge issue was gone. I could not muster any personal, negative reaction to this problem, and I felt cured. Now, I am not attributing my cure 100% to Tapping, but I became a believer in the power of healing the mind through energy work.

At first, it is somewhat unsettling with Tapping to focus on negativity. However, we do not realize how pervasive our negative thinking already is in our subconscious. By bringing the thoughts and emotions up and out of our automatic, subconscious world, we are able to make the negative known in our conscious mind, making the pain moldable.

Through Tapping, energy is unblocked. I have watched people begin with a SUDS measurement of a 9 or 10 out of 10. As the therapist and client start tapping, emotions can get so hot that the client sometimes cannot even repeat the statements to be said while tapping. Gradually, the continued tapping makes it easier to start speaking again. As they progress with the tapping, the emotional connection to the event or problem lessens. It really can be an amazing and powerful process.

Again, it is especially important that you not handle significantly stressful events or feelings (anything with a SUDS higher than a 6) without a trained therapist. It is important to not go into highly charged emotional areas alone. This is a reliving of pain from the past.

However, EFT is a fabulous tool for the downregulation of emotions. Do some research on EFT to gain a better understanding of the process. I highly recommend the Ortner family's work on EFT through their videos and presentations but mainly through the app called The Tapping Solution. Almost all physical ailments have an emotional component. Energy work basically removes the emotional reaction to pain, and healing begins.

EFT, EMDR, hypnosis, and many other techniques are all some form of working on issues at a deeper and more intuitive level. Traditional talk therapy can produce wonderful insights. The tools currently available with energy work though get to the real issues at a very accelerated speed compared to talk therapy. EFT is a tool to go back in time and heal from the source of the real issues. If you become triggered to past pain, please know there are many resources and tools available to therapists to help you resolve your emotional reactions to the past. A past filled with pain does not have to be a life sentence of pain.

Chapter Thirty-Five: Picture Therapy

I will neither confirm nor deny that my original purpose of taking up the art of scrapbooking was the hoarding of craft supplies. Now, fortunately, preserving memories is so much less about craft supplies but so much more about the joy of reliving memories.

My identity as a crafter provides me great meaning. I love all kinds of crafts. I am in my natural zone when I am crafting anything. The reality of my crafts is that I am not actually that good at it. I have needlepointed since I was a little girl, but needlepointing is really just having patience at following some rules of stitching. However, even though I am not fabulous at it, crafting is the one area of my life where I have let go of perfection. I can make mistakes. In fact, every new project is a test project with lower quality fabric because there are going to be tons of flaws.

When we are in our natural zone of talent, ironically the ego is not involved. We are using what God gave us. If anything, our talent is a testament of God's goodness. But, when we need others' validation for what we have produced, ego is all involved. Our value has been defined by how well we have performed a task. Our self-value should not be dependent on what we do but who we are. And, for those of faith, whose we are. So, I craft because it makes me so incredibly happy. Scrapbooking is one of the most freeing ways to craft our memories.

Have you ever had an awful hair day and decided to capture the image forever? Have you ever been sobbing after falling and suddenly stopped to take a selfie? We normally only bring out our cameras when we are happy. We want to record the happy moment in history by taking a picture.

When we are beating ourselves up about our past, we tend to focus only on the negatives. We forget that we were good to ourselves, that there were good times, and that we were happy. Pictures are wonderful reminders to balance the playing field a bit on our look backs to the past.

This is why I have been a scrapbooker and cheerleader for everyone to use their photos in everyday life. Make calendars that are daily reminders of good times last year. Place photos on mirrors and the refrigerator of times when you were thinner. If you were there once, you can be there again. (My hair stylist told me that frequently people bring in pictures of celebrities for her to copy. She wishes people would bring her pictures of themselves with hair styles they liked on themselves. You do not need to look like someone else to feel good.) While we should not live in the past, our pictures are a way to negate the negative self-talk that plays like a broken record in our minds.

I have a photo of me in my wedding dress a few days before my wedding. I could spend (and have spent) a long time studying that picture. No, this is not a confession of my vanity, but I just laugh every time I see it. You see, the photographer suggested my mother and I do a rehearsal with my makeup, hair, and dress a few days before the wedding for the bride's photos. My mother was my matron of honor, and those pictures with her are treasures of mine. My photographer explained that a bride's photos are usually so relaxed because they are not taken on the hectic day of the wedding. I study one particular photo because it is a picture of me holding my long train in one hand and my bouquet in another, with my eyes closed. I was standing on a small bridge at a hotel in my hometown. There was a koi pond beneath the bridge, and the photographer had just asked me to twirl around in my dress on the bridge for a photo effect. Earlier as we were walking onto the bridge, I mentioned to my mother that I was feeling dizzy. I had not eaten lunch yet, and I had been on an insane diet that made me very weak.

I stare at that picture and laugh because it is as if I can hear my mother on the sidelines telling the photographer, "That's a wrap. We are all done." My mom was convinced I was going to fall off that bridge in my weakened state and ruin my dress among the koi. As my mom is begging the photographer to stop, the photographer keeps telling me to twirl. Here I am an adult stuck between two bosses yelling the opposite directions to me. Not only was that day hysterical, but I get the opportunity to relive that moment with each view of that photo. That is exactly what happens when our minds relive our past, but our minds are usually reliving pain.

Picture therapy is using our happiest of times to level the playing field and remember the good times. It puts our past pain into perspective, especially as our minds can play tricks on us. Use your pictures. As a side note, the photographer absolutely loved the picture over the bridge so much that she made a gigantic copy of it for her second floor studio. She hung that picture in the hallway, and everyone saw it as they ascended the stairs to her office. After several years of hanging the large picture in her office, my mom purchased that photo. After my mom moved and was unable to hang that photo in her new home, guess who was the benefactor of said photo. When it has been displayed in our home, I have had fun telling people the back story. This is one back story I don't mind telling.

Travel back in time. Use your photos as a way to relive the joys of being free from work, from worries, and from responsibilities. The goal of working on our past is to travel to the future with the lessons of the past, not the pain. When we change our emotional connection to the pain and focus on what the takeaways are, we are using every bit of where we have been. In my Strengths Awareness testing through Gallup, a two-word combination of my top five strengths is a Curious Historian. The shadow side of being a Curious Historian is a tendency to stay in the past. However, I have done most of the work on my past already. I know the triggers and red flags. I have learned rich lessons from my past. My bags are packed for a bright future.

Like the story of the donkey who is stuck in the hole, use the earth that is thrown to bury you as your way of lifting you out of the hole. (The story goes that the farmer could not get the donkey out of a hole and decided to throw down earth to bury him and to put him out of his misery. The donkey used that earth to pat down and to lift him out of his problem.) What we mistakenly thought was given to destroy us could become our greatest asset. The money spent on vacations can give the greatest return of value by reliving the joys vacations bring.

Use your pictures as a way to keep the positive memories alive. Keep traveling back to all of your happy places.

Chapter Thirty-Six: The Blessing of Anxiety

What? Really? A blessing? That is going out on quite a limb because I imagine anxiety does not feel like a blessing EVER. But, yes, anxiety can be seen as a blessing if you change your vision of it. Think of anxiety like a fever. There is an indication that something is wrong. Without that indication, you might just become apathetic to your past and cynical that life is just that awful. Life is not awful. Terrible things may have happened to you in the past, but it is in the PAST. How you've processed those terrible things needs to be reviewed, changed, and refined. The abuse, trauma, sadness, and loneliness are not eternal. You can learn the lessons.

That is why the company that I founded is called The Learning Club. It is called a club to highlight inclusion and focus toward a common goal of learning our lessons. We have rich volumes of lessons to learn from out past. (Countries and the whole world too can learn from the past, which is why we study history.) Everything that happens to us is an opportunity to learn. However, it is as much The Unlearning Club as it is The Learning Club. There are ample lessons from our past that need to be unlearned as well.

For those who are having a hard time coping with life, they develop WA's (Work Arounds). They have adapted their environment and their actions to ease the anxiety symptoms. They start doing rituals, they stop going outside, and they shut down the regular parts of life. Soon though, those safety procedures are less and less effective. That is when they usually seek professional help. When they initially hear in therapy that those WA methods will have to be eliminated, there is a lot of fear and rightly so. The therapist is suggesting to take away their carefully crafted coping mechanisms.

What will be the replacement? It is a removal of the emotional investment into trauma or pain and a focus on a new meaning that makes you happy. In as much as anxiety sufferers want control, these coping mechanisms are a temporary way to control their environment to be able to function. But, as I have seen time and time again, the coping mechanisms soon become the problem instead of the solution. Instead, the answer is to go back in time and solve the real problem. So, yes, anxiety is the brain's way of protecting itself from something that is wrong. While anxiety seeks control, your thoughts are entirely within your control. By listening to your thoughts, learning your values, triggers, and red flags, trusting yourself, telling the truth, writing your story of the past and your future story, and then changing that story, you will be treating that mind's fever, the anxiety.

If I never had the obsessive thoughts, the compulsive behaviors, the inability to let go, and the lack of self-forgiveness in my life, I never would have been able to really understand anxiety. I would not have been able to understand others' pain and to help them. I would not have been able to write this book. So, while it was really hard work to kick mind clutter to the curb, I am grateful for anxiety's lessons. I am living proof that peace of mind is an exceptionally good thing that everyone can have.

NO MATTER WHAT has happened to you in the past, change your story.

Acknowledgments

I would first like to thank Boy. Boy was my imaginary friend who traveled everywhere with me. At an early age, I would stop dinner conversations with the adults to say, "Wait, what was that, Boy?" I miss Boy, but that is on me because he is always with me. I just need to invite him over more. Boy actually represents all of the guardian angels in my life. Yes, I really do need to turn to them more and let them into my life. Thank you for always being here with me.

I want to thank all of those amazing people who have shared their stories with me. Oh, how I love a good story!

I want to thank the people who pushed me to tackle my demons, even though I was kicking and screaming. Usually, my greatest growth begins with me kicking and screaming.

I want to thank those who love to laugh with me. Did you hear that preposition I used? WITH me, AT me is an entirely different thing. Actually, when I am able to laugh at myself is when I feel the most me because I am loving all parts of myself. Try it; it is good for the soul.

Thanks to those who showed me they are having fun by hanging out with me for no other reason than it's me.

I want to thank those people who walked right by me as if I didn't exist, who never invited me to their parties, who never made me a member of their club, and who forced me to stop wanting what would never make me better.

I want to thank all of those who share their lessons with everyone, mostly you YouTubers who teach. To you crafters who generously post videos to help expand others' world, my homemade (from a video) hat is off to you! Thank you to all of those self-help authors for putting yourself in not such a grand light in order to teach a difficult lesson. I have read so many self-help books that I should write one. Oh, I guess I just did.

Made in the USA
Middletown, DE
12 July 2020

12623185R00086